Wisdom With
Understanding
is Better
Than Rubies

Lurine Karon Greenberg
Fine Arts Collection

Shawnee Pottery

An Identification & Value Guide

Jim and Bev Mangus

COLLECTOR BOOKS

A Division of Schroeder Publishing Co., Inc.

The current values in this book should be used only as a guide. They are not intended to set prices, which vary from one section of the country to another. Auction prices as well as dealer prices vary greatly and are affected by condition as well as demand. Neither the authors nor the publisher assumes responsibility for any losses that might be incurred as a result of consulting this guide.

Searching For A Publisher?

We are always looking for knowledgeable people considered to be experts within their fields. If you feel that there is a real need for a book on your collectible subject and have a large comprehensive collection, contact Collector Books.

ON THE COVER:
Bud Vase, $12.00–14.00; Fruit Casserole, marked Shawnee USA 83, $40.00–45.00, Dolphin, marked USA, $8.00–10.00; Cottage, 5 cup, marked USA7, $350.00+; Jumbo, $55.00–60.00; Caboose, marked USA 553, $45.00–50.00; Box Car, marked USA 552, $45.00–50.00; Coal Car (Oops! car was reversed when photographed), marked USA 551, $45.00–50.00; Train Engine, marked USA 550, $45.00–50.00.

COVER DESIGN: Sherry Kraus
BOOK DESIGN: Beth Ray
BOOK LAYOUT: Bev Mangus

COLLECTOR BOOKS
P.O. Box 3009
Paducah, Kentucky 42002-3009

DEDICATION

To our Parents

Kenes and Alice Logan
and
Anthony and Adeline Mangus

To our Daughter

Ami

Thank you for your love and support

ACKNOWLEDGMENTS

Three years ago, this book was just a dream. To all of our old friends and to the many new ones that we have made through this endeavor, we want to thank you for helping to make a dream come true.

To my sister, Lisa Logan Pariano, I love you, and I want to thank you for being there for me when I needed you.

A very special thank you to Don and Margaret Merryman. The knowledge that you have shared with us is invaluable. We treasure your friendship and will be forever grateful for all you have taught us.

Our thanks to Duane and Janice Vanderbilt, you were always there for us. We came to rely on your encouragement and support, which, by the way, was never ending.

Thank you, Cecil and Mary Rapp; you opened your home to us and unselfishly shared, not only your extensive knowledge, but many wonderful pieces of Shawnee.

To Rich and Linda Guffey, we thank you, not only for hauling pottery from California to Ohio for us but also for packing and shipping more pottery than any of us care to think about. Most importantly though, we thank you for your friendship.

A very warm thanks to Elvin Culp of Clara Belles Antiques in Zanesville. You have been a good friend to us from the beginning. You're always kind, always generous, and always willing to take the time to help us learn.

We also would like to thank the following people who allowed us to photograph their pottery, supplied us with needed information, or helped us with the pricing:

Dan and Kathy Ahlstedt
Carlos and Marlene Allen
Icel Ball
Louise Bauer
Terry and Sandy Bauer
Ron and Connie Brown
Bill and Ruth Bywater
Harvey Duke
Sharon Figura
Lee Foster
Ryan Guffey
Tom and Norma Harmon
Tim and Kate Joseph
Kathy Kenez

Juan and Bonita Klinehoffer
Ralph Meranto
Kevin and Billie Mills
Chuck Newton
Jim and Bev Novonglosky
Dean and Sue Page
Claude and Ruth Reed
Norris Schneider
Linda Spenst
Gary Streit
Denise Teeters
Bernard Twiggs
Eleanor Twiggs
Charles (Chic) and Betty Willey

Photography by Jim Mangus
Arrowhead logo trademark owned by Beverly Mangus

TABLE OF CONTENTS

INTRODUCTION

In the 24 years that the Shawnee Pottery Company was in operation, it manufactured thousands of different pieces of pottery. Our intent was to cover as many of these as possible. We realize that many pieces were poured from identical molds and decorated in a variety of ways, and it is not uncommon to find collectors seeking the same piece, in different colors and with different decals. In order to picture as many different pieces as possible, we were forced to eliminate some of the color and/or decal variations. The decision to exclude a variation was never an easy one for us; however, we believe the sacrifice was worth the opportunity to include some of the pottery that has never before been shown.

Where possible, we have used the proper name of the piece from information gathered through catalogs and advertising pamphlets.

Sizes are included where necessary; however, due to the amount of shrinkage when a piece of pottery is fired and the size difference when new molds were made, you will find that measurements may differ from ¼" to ½" from what is stated.

We hope you enjoy the book and hope it displays Shawnee Pottery's beauty and versatility.

PRICING

The prices in this book represent current market value. As prices vary in different parts of the country according to availability, we gathered the pricing information geographically from shows, flea markets, dealers, trade papers, and collectors. Prices are for pieces in mint condition. Pottery with chips and/or cracks will bring considerably less. Gold trimmed and decorated pieces will bring approximately 40% to 50% more. The prices in this book should only be used as a guide.

REMINISCING

The favorite part of our research has been the opportunity to talk with former employees of the Shawnee Pottery Company. They all have been very gracious and generous with their time and information. We would like to share a small part of their lives with you.

Sitting in the living room with Bernard Twiggs and his daughter Eleanor was an honor for us. Even though we had just met, we immediately felt comfortable and knew we would become friends.

Bernard started to work at Shawnee in 1937, made 59 cents an hour, and remained there until its closing in 1961. He was hired as a Block and Caser, and after six months became Supervisor of the Mold and Dye Room. Bernard's father, Clifton Twiggs, worked at Roseville Pottery, and his Uncle, Clifford Twiggs, worked at Shawnee. Prior to his employment at Shawnee, Bernard had been working at the Roseville Pottery company since the age of 17.

Bernard was able to help us identify some pieces that we had taken to show him. He also told us about items that we did not know were Shawnee. Through his description we were able to find some of these pieces and photograph them for the book. Because he is a very modest man, it took Eleanor to show us just how talented her father is. Bernard is also a very skilled wood worker. We had the privilege to see some beautiful pieces of furniture he made and some hand carved figures that were remarkable.

Listening to him describe the factory and what it was like to work there was a thrill for us. Thank you, Bernard and Eleanor, for welcoming us in your home.

Spending an afternoon with Icel Ball is nothing short of delightful. She is the mother of fellow collector Marlene Allen. Icel was the 50th employee hired at Shawnee in 1937. She remained there until 1946. Her late husband Guy Ball was employed at Shawnee from 1939 until 1961.

For the first two years Icel cleaned greenware, after which she was promoted to a decorator. She remembers the first piece she decorated was a teapot with red flowers. A check mark was scratched in the bottom of the teapot, to identify it. After it was fired, the foreman pulled the teapot to make sure the decorating technique was appropriate, and it was then given to her. The teapot now sits proudly in Marlene's collection.

Icel explained to us that all of the piece workers were assigned a number, which they would ink stamp on the bottom of each piece. The items were counted, and the employees were paid accordingly. As a decorator, she would sometimes be required to use gold. She told us that a bottle of gold was one gram, and because of the expense, it had to be signed out in the morning and signed back in before they went home.

We were surprised when Icel mentioned that there was a dress code for the factory workers. The women were required to wear white dresses, or white skirts and blouses, and the men were required to wear white shirts and pants.

We would like to thank you for inviting us to your home, and sharing your memories with us.

Louise Bauer started to work for Shawnee as a designer in 1937 and remained there for 3½ years. Like Bernard, Louise grew up in a pottery family. Her father worked for more than 20 years as a designer and worker in clay products. He had a small shop adjoining his home, which is where Louise got her start. She remembers, as a child, helping her dad design and turn pottery.

Louise is responsible for designing the Arrowhead logo, the Valencia dinnerware line, the Scotty Dog wallpocket, most of the miniatures that are pictured in this book, and numerous planters and vases.

She left her position at Shawnee to become one of the few independent women pottery designers in the country. She later went to work at the Hull Pottery Factory and remained there until its closing. Louise has designed hundreds of items, for companies all over the country. Her contribution to the pottery industry is second to none.

Thank you, Louise, for sharing so many of your afternoons and so much valuable information with us.

THE SHAWNEE POTTERY COMPANY

The Shawnee Pottery company began operations in 1937 in Zanesville, Ohio. The trademark of the company was an arrowhead with a profile of a Shawnee Indian on it. Malcolm A. Schweiker was inspecting the grounds of the old American Encaustic Tiling Company plant in 1937 to convert the buildings to the manufacture of pottery by a new company. As he was thinking about a name for the new organization, he happened to see an Indian arrowhead on the ground. That was not surprising, because an Indian skeleton with flint weapons and tools had been uncovered when the plant was under construction in 1891.

Schweiker consulted the history books to see what tribes had lived along the Muskingum and had probably made the arrowhead he found. He learned that the Shawnee tribe of Indians once made the land adjoining the bank of the Muskingum River their home. A Shawnee village is believed to have been located on the site where the factory is located. The Shawnee Indians were probably the first craftsmen in the area, and produced pottery from Zanesville clays long before the area was settled by others. The arrowhead in the trademark is a duplicate of the one found in the area. The name was easily pronounced and associated with the trademark. Consumers remembered the trademark from seeing it on products and in consumer advertising.

The Shawnee Pottery Company opened the plant of the old American Encaustic Company, which was once the largest tile works in the world. The large building was constructed in 1891. It was dedicated by Governor William McKinley on April 19, 1892. It cost nearly a million dollars. For three decades or more, it was known throughout the world for its famed mosaics which adorn many of the greatest buildings in the world. American Encaustic gradually failed during the depression and closed its doors in 1935. The Youngstown Sheet and Tube Company plant in Putnam had stopped production in 1930. The Brown Manufacturing Company and the Harris and Burton-Townsend brick factories had ceased operations in the preceding decade. The industrial picture of the city was gloomy.

The people of Zanesville cheered in 1937 at the announcement that the newly organized Shawnee Pottery Company would take over the old American Encaustic works for the manufacture of pottery. Many skilled and unskilled clay workers were unemployed. News of the new plant was encouraging.

The factory was located at 2200 Lindin Avenue, in Zanesville, Ohio. The Lindin Avenue works consisted of 50 buildings on 40 acres of ground. The floor space covered over 650,000 square feet, which is approximately 15 acres, and was capable of producing 100,000 pieces of pottery a day.

At the time of purchase, the plant contained 25 periodic kilns, three large harrop car tunnels, decorating kilns, and test kilns. It was proposed that 22 of the periodic kilns be removed as they were not advantageous for the proposed method of pottery manufacturing.

Zanesville was in the largest pottery manufacturing area in the United States. Other than kitchenware the Zanesville district manufactured more pottery than all of the surrounding districts combined. Pottery manufacturing had been in this area for generations. The factory's location was quite favorable, because Zanesville was located between the Eastern and Midwestern markets, which comprised the largest markets in the country. The principal customers of the company were chain stores and department stores located in cities east of the Rocky Mountains. The Zanesville location was such that quick deliveries could be made to all of these important markets. Another advantage of the location was the available shipping facilities. Zanesville is located at the junction of the Licking and Muskingum Rivers. This enabled water transportation to the Ohio River Valley. Through these two main waterways, access was gained to the New Orleans gateway into Texas and alternately the Pacific Coast ports. The property had railroad shipping facilities through belt line connections with four railroads: New York Central, Baltimore and Ohio, Pennsylvania, and Wheeling and Lake Erie.

Addis E. Hull, Jr. was president and general manager of the Shawnee Pottery Company at the time of its organization in 1937. For six years he had been president and general manager of the A.E. Hull Pottery of Crooksville, which had been founded by his father. He resigned from his position at Hull to head the new Shawnee Company.

Robert Shilling became vice president and treasurer of the new company. He had been associated with the American Encaustic Tiling Company and for several years was in complete charge of manufacturing operations.

Ernest B. Graham of Zanesville was secretary, and J. Brannon Hull was general sales manager. Directors included Addis Hull, Jr., Robert Shilling, W. Herbert Keller of Norristown, Pennsylvania, Maurice Isernam of New York City, and Malcolm A. Schweiker.

When the Shawnee company started operation in 1937, this country was beginning to feel hostility towards Germany and Japan and their imports. "Buy American" campaigns were conducted. The chain stores were forced to look for American sources for their pottery.

The designs for the products originally made were supplied by S.S. Kresge Company, F.W. Woolworth Company, and the McCrory stores. These companies provided the original designs and promised to purchase their requirements if the items could be made. George Schwerber, who had worked for S.A. Weller Company, modeled the pieces, and Clifford Twiggs, who had learned his trade at the Roseville Pottery Company, made the blocks or dies and cases.

Within a few months Sears Roebuck and Company sent their housewares stylist, Jane Miller, a merchandise manager, F. R. Henniger, and their pottery buyer, James Butler, to Zanesville to help Shawnee design a dinnerware and kitchenware line for them. Combining their efforts with Louise Bauer, a designer for Shawnee, the Valencia dinnerware was created. These orders further helped the new company get started.

In April 1938 George RumRill moved his production from Red Wing Pottery Company to Shawnee. His line was a fancy pottery line which competed with Weller and Roseville. Mr. Rum-Rill supplied the designs, and Schwerber and Twiggs did the modeling and block and casing.

At first Shawnee manufactured ware designed by customers. Then it was decided that the company should have its own designer to plan lines for general sale. Mr. Hull heard of a young German, who was a designer for the Frankoma Pottery Company, and previously had been carving names on tombstones in Fort Smith, Arkansas. His name was Rudy Ganz. He had come from Germany in 1928 and studied at Indiana University. He came to Shawnee as a designer and remained for five years.

Another designer in the early years of the Shawnee operation was Louise Bauer, a graduate from Columbus College of Art and Design. Louise assisted in designing the Valencia dinnerware and many of the other early pieces. Louise left Shawnee after 3½ years to design for the Hull Pottery Company.

Shawnee grew rapidly. By 1940 the company employed 450 people. At the close of 1939 the annual payroll was figured at $500,000.

In 1942 Ed Hazel joined the designing department and remained for two years. He resigned to help organize the Cordelia China Company of Dalton, Ohio. To supervise manufacturing of the lines, George C. Earle became plant superintendent when the plant was purchased and remained until production was started. Then George Frauenfelter became superintendent and served in that position until 1949.

From 1937 to 1942 many types of pottery were made. The company initially manufactured pottery products that had a low production cost and were simple in design.

Some of the various types of pottery manufactured were:

A. Chain Stores: Fancy pottery, vases, flower pots, flower bowls and dish planters, figurines, jardinieres, and kitchenware pottery, mostly tea pots
B. Dinnerware and kitchenware for Sears Roebuck and kitchenware for general jobbers
C. Fancy pottery for RumRill and florists jobbers
D. Lamp bases for lamp manufactures
E. Special items for premium trade, such as coffee pots, cookie jars, creamers, sugars, and mixing bowls. The largest account was Proctor and Gamble for premiums.

The retail price of the various products manufactured ranged from 10 cents to a dollar, but the majority retailed between 10 cents and 30 cents per piece.

The ware was sold to these nationally known retailers, which also operated stores in Zanesville: S. S. Kresge Company of Detroit, Michigan, F. W. Woolworth Company of New York City, J.J. Newberry Company of New York City, Sears Roebuck and Company of Chicago, and Montgomery Ward and Company of Chicago. Other nationally known retailers were: McCrory Stores Corporation of New York City, H.L. Green Company of New York City, G. C. Murphy Company of McKeesport, Pennsylvania, S.H. Kress and Company of New York City, Neisner Brother Inc. of Rochester, New York, McClellan Stores of New York City, Butler Brothers of Chicago, Keller Whilldin Pottery of North Wales, Pennsylvania, and Hermann Brothers of Detroit. Ware was also manufactured on order, such as lamp bases for the Industrial Studio of Brooklyn and coffee pots for Aluminum Enterprise Company of Massillion, Ohio.

These large retail outlets and jobbers distributed Zanesville-made pottery to all parts of the United States and to a number of foreign countries, thus spreading the pottery fame of Zanesville to millions of persons.

Shawnee was one of the first local plants to receive war contracts. In October 1942, company officials announced that additional people would be employed to operate a new department using the patented Formrite process. The product consisted of jigs, dies, molds, patterns, and fixtures for aviation and automotive industries. The new process saved half the time previously needed to make dies and molds. In making Formrite a powder and a liquid were mixed under a vacuum for 45 minutes to produce a creamy substance, which was poured into a mold to produce as many duplicates of a part as needed.

The Army Air Force rented the southern part of the Shawnee plant in April, 1943 for a depot to receive, store, maintain, modify, and ship Army Air Force materials throughout the world. Orders were received from distant parts of the world by mail, teletype, and telephone.

During the war the Army Air Force took over the entire plant, except the power house, machine shop, and sagger shop. The use of the Formrite process was discontinued in early 1943.

In July 1945, the 833rd Army Air Force depot was open to the public for the first time on Army Air Force day. Visitors saw parts being crated and prepared for shipment. An interesting feature was the corrosion control unit of the packaging branch. Six hundred workers were employed. The depot kept 8,000 items in stock. They ranged from small parts to a three-ton lathe.

Major George J. Klein was in command of the depot. His office was the former American Encaustic Tiling Company show room. The elaborate tile decorations were valued at $50,000. A fountain designed by Frederick Rhead was the focal point of the room. It included the black and gold figure of a boy modeled by Lois Rhead, wife of the designer. Emma Hale, who decorated most of the tile used in construction of the fountain, was employed at the Army Air Force depot.

After V-E Day, May 8, 1945, the need for the established defense quickly decreased. Officials of the Shawnee Pottery Company made formal application on October 28, 1945, for the return of the buildings occupied by the AAF. The Army conducted sales of its surplus materials in 1946, and in July the plant was returned to the Shawnee Company.

In the limited space available to them during the period that the AAF occupied the factory, Shawnee officials were only able to retain some of their key personnel to test and develop modern methods of making pottery. Little manufacturing of pottery for domestic use was done during the war emergency. Full time operations of the Shawnee plant were resumed in 1946. There was a pent up demand for pottery, and within 2 years Shawnee employed 250 people.

In 1950 Malcolm A. Schweiker sold his interest in the Shawnee Pottery Company to a syndicate in Philadelphia. In the same year Addis Hull resigned from the presidency of the company and was succeeded by Albert P. Braid as president.

Faced with increasing foreign and domestic competition a decade before, Shawnee joined the trend to the manufacture of decorated flower pots, "cute" planters, and various other novelties. The market was overcrowded with this type of ware; as a result, the sales declined substantially, and the company suffered a severe operating loss in 1954.

On September 1, 1954, John F. Bonistall arrived at Shawnee as executive vice president and general manager. John Bonistall attended the University of Pittsburgh and served in the U.S. Army during World War II. He was elected president and a member of the board of directors three months after his arrival. Key personnel had been leaving Shawnee, because the plant appeared to be headed for disaster. Bonistall, who was without experience in the manufacturing of pottery, took charge. His insistence that members of his new executive staff and sales force have no previous experience in the manufacture of pottery caused more employees to quit, but those who remained, soon belonged to a growing and prosperous concern.

Bonistall introduced many revolutionary ideas. Faced with the necessity of out-designing and out-merchandising the Japanese, he abolished hand decorating and substituted the spray gun. To reduce costs he mechanized many operations. For exterior finishes on some lines he substituted the products of the industrial finishes for ceramic glazes. They produced unusual finishes in beautiful color tones. In design, as well as manufacturing methods, Bonistall was original and revolutionary. His aim was to create lines that would be American in appearance rather than Oriental or European, which would imply good taste, rather than the bizarre, ornate, or overdecorated.

His first Art Line, the most successful in the history of Shawnee, was Touché. Other successful art lines were Liana, Fairy Wood, Chantilly, Petit-Point, Fernware, Cameo, and Elegance. Some miscellaneous items were casseroles, chafing dishes, clocks, console sets, lazy susans, bathroom accessories, ashtrays, and designs such as Monte Carlo, Studio, Artique, Riviera, Hostess, and Flight.

Bonistall's innovations in manufacture and design were able not only to sell pottery in competition with foreign imports but also to produce gift shop type ware at mass-market prices. Under John Bonistall's leadership Shawnee Pottery once again became one of the largest pottery manufacturers in the country.

The Shawnee Pottery Company was forced to close its doors in 1961. After much effort without compromising the quality of their wares, Shawnee was no longer able to compete with the cost of the foreign pottery that was being imported.

Shawnee Devises A Method To Speed Up Production 1940

Zanesville was a world known clay center. It provided a livelihood for several thousands of persons. Each person took pride in the various steps of the manufacture of pottery, and his or her artistry was developed through practice and patience in such an industry.

Pottery designates any article made or formed of baked or burned clay. Consequently, the product varies from the finest eggshell china to the roughest paving brick and includes tile, dinnerware, stoneware, porcelain, vitreous and encaustic ware, and other like materials.

Earthenware is characterized by a solid ring, or musical note, when solidly struck. It is made of white materials and after the first firing becomes a solid white, opaque ware which is usually not vitreous, or hard.

For both utility and decoration earthenware generally is covered with a thin solution known as glaze, which forms a veneer or covering of glass, practically always of some color or combination of colors. Application and burning of glaze on ware gives the surface a vitreous covering which protects the soft body from wear, and at the same time the interior glaze prevents seepage of liquids through the porous material. Generally, the ware was burned first to make the body, and the glaze was then applied to the piece and burned a second time. However, Shawnee employed a method of producing ware with one firing.

Materials used in the manufacture of pottery could be divided into five different groups, the ware, of course, varied with the composition of materials employed. They may be described roughly as follows:

1. Clay, consisting of ball clay and China clay or kaolin
2. China stone of various kinds
3. Flint
4. Feldspar
5. Bone, and various coloring agents, such as barium or cobalt oxide

The mixture of these materials determined the type and even the quality of the finished product. The proportions also determined whether the body would be opaque, earthenware, vitreous earthenware, or bone china. Ball clay was seldom used in making china; it was not as good as china clay.

The recipe for earthenware depended on several things. First, the body must be pliable enough to be easily worked into the various shapes required. The ware must not contract or shrink too much from the original design, and it must be infusible enough to prevent collapse in the firing kiln. Another important requirement is purity from dirt and especially iron, which would tint the ware brown in the firing. The glaze, which gave the ware a vitreous covering, must be free flowing and translucent. It also must be so balanced that it would not change or injure colors added to it. The coefficient of the expansion of the body and the glaze must be equal, or blisters would form on the ware, or the glaze would crack or craze.

Finally, a very efficient test was made of all batches of ingredients, whether they came from the same mine or from separate parts of the world. One carload of clay may have been different from another carload taken from the same clay pit.

The pottery market varied greatly in the United States, and while a great many of the industries catered to the wealthier class of trade, others found a great field for consumption of lower priced ware of good quality and workmanship.

To place ware in the lower price bracket, it had to be made in a modern and efficient plant in which production was speeded by modern mechanical methods. Shawnee fell into this classification. Higher priced earthenware was fired first to bake the bisque or body and then fired a second time to fuse the glaze. If an overglaze was desired, it was fired a third time. Overglazes generally were confined to expensive wall tile. Although most potteries fired their ware twice, Shawnee found that it could produce excellent ware at a lower cost than other companies by only firing once. However, all the ware was thoroughly dried before glaze was applied.

Once-fired pottery was produced with difficulty and some sacrifice of original shape, and with blisters, crazes, and pitted surfaces. The methods that Shawnee employed minimized these defects to a point where the pottery was produced with very few, if any, defects and sold at lower costs on a high production schedule.

Three distinct pottery innovations were employed at Shawnee. The first deviation in the method of manufacture was the manner of preparation of clay to be used in the body. Most potteries generally pulverized the clay and added water until a slip was formed. Later it was dried in filter presses and then made into great cakes. The clay also was screened and freed from metallic deposits by the use of a giant magnet.

At Shawnee, the pottery clay was washed to remove lignite, a type of soft combustible mineral, which occasionally entered the clay deposit in the mining process. Unless the lignite was removed, it would burn out in the kiln firing of the clay, leaving holes and also pitting the ware where the gaseous vapors escaped.

Clay received at the Shawnee company was handled by electrically controlled buckets, operating on a single overhead tramway, and the cost of moving it into bins and vats was minimized. The clay was prepared in dry form and passed under heavy muller wheels and plows that mixed and blended the materials, while a spray of water moistened it to the desired consistency. Consequently, the expensive filter press operation was eliminated.

The prepared jigger clay also passed through an auger machine and then through a de-airing machine with a vacuum from 25 to 29 inches of mercury. In the partial vacuum practically all of the air in the clay was removed. If too much air remained in the body when fired, bubbles and small pinholes would appear in the finished product where the air escaped in the intense heat of the firing kilns. This finished mixture made an ideal jigger clay.

A second deviation from the older methods of pottery manufacture was the method of jiggering or molding of regularly shaped pieces. The jigger was used in the manufacture of pottery, where the interior was of regular or round shape, and in which no corners were required. The jigger also was used to manufacture pottery in which the opening was large enough to allow entrance of a hand, blade, or a knife.

To set up production in the jiggering department, a large machine was invented by Shawnee engineers. This consisted of a large drying oven of about 150 feet in length. At one end two jiggermen shaped the ware in molds which were supplied to them by two other men, called "ballers-in" who placed a ball of clay in the molds. Through experience they learned the exact amount of clay required by the jiggerman, who shaped the ware in the mold.

The jiggerman set the mold with the wet clay on the slowly moving belt which passed through the drying ovens. At the other end of the belt, was another man designated the "off-bearer." It was his task to remove the dried ware from the mold and set it up for four women who would sponge the ware to remove defects such as pimples, strings, and other marks which may have been inadvertently caused by handling or jiggering. The "off-bearer" then placed the emptied mold on the endless belt which carried it back to the "ballers-in" who again filled the mold for the jiggerman. The process could be continued 24 hours a day and until the mold was worn out.

It was estimated that 10,000 pieces of ware could be jiggered on this ingenious machine in eight hours, the equivalent of 1,500 pieces an hour. The machine was six times as fast as the ordinary method, and consequently, only one sixth as many molds were required. In most potteries the jiggerman filled his own mold and set it on boards or trays which were carried away, and allowed to dry for up to 24 hours. That involved, added operation expense in carrying the ware from the jiggerman to the dryer and also required a much larger number of molds.

The ware jiggered at the Shawnee plant passed through a steam dryer in the drying kiln. The belt carried it from the jiggerman to the "off-bearer" in an hour and 20 minutes. It should be understood that the hourly production of ware depended to some extent on the size and shape of the piece being jiggered.

The third innovation of the production method at Shawnee was the mechanical process employed in the slip molding method of ware manufacture. Equipment in the building of the old American Encaustic Tiling Company was altered extensively by the Shawnee engineers. A 500 feet tramway was added. The molds were placed on trays suspended from the traveling tram, and as they would pass one station, an employee filled the mold to a certain depth by means of a flexible tube with a hand controlled valve.

The advantage of this plan over other methods is easily understood. In other potteries a molder walked past the molds, and as they sat in rows, he filled them from a bucket with a small spout.

At Shawnee, the molds passed through a long steam-heated oven, at the opposite end of which the molds were opened, and the ware removed. When the ware dried, it was placed in front of other employees who sponged off defects or trimmed mold marks. When the mold was emptied, it was placed back on the moving tram, which returned to the first station for refilling. This method also greatly reduced the number of molds required and also the time for drying. The mold was made of plaster of paris, a porous substance which absorbs the moisture from the "slip" and at the same time draws the clay against the side of the mold. When sufficient clay forms against the side of the mold, the remainder was poured out into a stainless steel trough, which returned excess slip to a reservoir for reconditioning and reuse. The removal of the excess slip was completed at one of the stations on the moving tram.

When the ware, both molded and jiggered pieces, was sufficiently dried and sponged of defects and trimmed of marks, it was dipped in large vats of glaze prepared at the plant. The process was completed by hand and by machine, depending upon the design and size. Spray guns, operated in protected booths, also were used at the Shawnee plant.

After the greenware was dipped in the glaze vats, it was placed in saggers, and they were passed through tunnel kilns and were fired at about 1980 degrees Fahrenheit. They were fired only once and when sufficiently cooled, were sorted and taken to the packing room and prepared for shipment. Shawnee's ware was carefully packed in corrugated paper boxes that were manufactured locally, or crated and prepared for delivery.

Products of Shawnee Pottery could be described as quality merchandise manufactured for a quick turnover. Consequently, it was manufactured on a production basis at less cost and prices within the means of the ordinary family.

LABELS

How many times have we picked up a piece of pottery with no company name on it? More times than we care to remember. We say to ourselves, "The color looks right, the glaze seems right, and the weight feels good, but there is no way to know for sure." Many different pottery companies marked their pottery USA. This USA mark became especially popular during the war to show the company's patriotism. Also, a type USA marking was required, if the pottery was to be shipped out of the country. Paper labels were also frequently used; unfortunately not many lasted over the years. The following are a few examples of some of the paper labels used by Shawnee.

Cameo   Cherie   Coaster/Ashtray

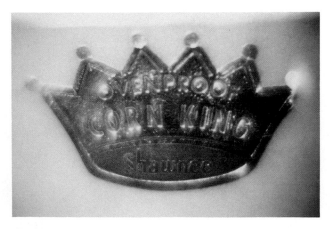

Corn King

Darn Aid

Elegance

Essex China

Fairy Wood

Kenwood

Liana

Petit-Point

Sample

Stardust

Tiara

Touché

Shawnee

Shawnee

PLANTERS

The following pages contain different planter designs. It is not uncommon to find many of these planters in a variety of different colors.

Kitten
Marked: USA 723
$32.00 – 35.00

Cat and Sax
Marked: USA 729
$32.00 – 35.00

Kitten and Basket
Marked: Shawnee USA 2026
$30.00 – 32.00

Cat
Marked: USA
$12.00 – 15.00

Lying Dog
Marked: USA
$12.00 – 15.00

Sitting Dog
Marked: USA
$12.00 – 15.00

Puppy with Fly
No Mark
$12.00 – 15.00

Poodle and Carriage
Marked: USA 704
$32.00 – 35.00

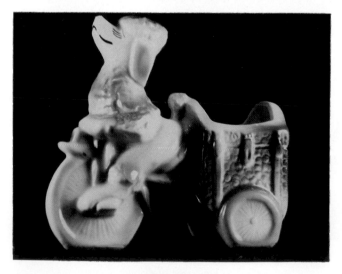

Poodle on Bicycle
Marked: USA 712
$32.00 – 35.00

Spaniel and Dog House
Marked: Shawnee USA
$22.00 – 25.00

Terrier and Dog House
Marked: Shawnee USA
$22.00 – 25.00

Chihuahua and Dog House
Marked: Shawnee USA
$22.00 – 25.00

Dog in a Boat
Marked: Shawnee 736
$30.00 – 35.00

Two Dogs/Gold
Marked: USA 611
$18.00 – 20.00

Dog and Jug
Marked: USA 610
$8.00 – 10.00

Irish Setter
Marked: USA
$8.00 – 10.00

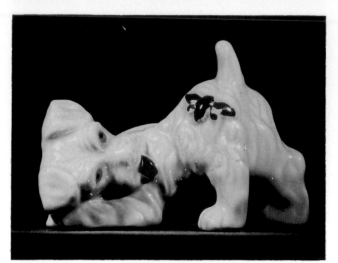

Embossed Puppy and Fly
Marked: USA
$12.00 – 15.00

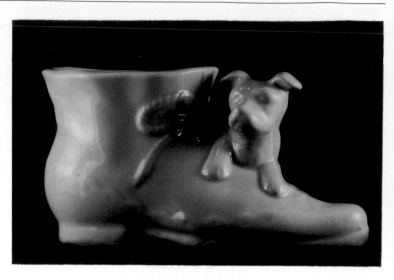

Shoe and Dog 2 Button
Marked: USA
$10.00 – 12.00

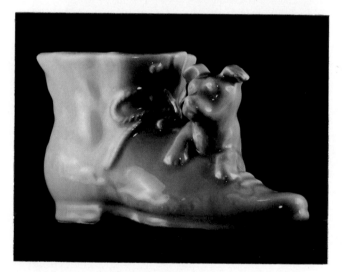

Shoe and Dog 3 Button
Marked: USA
$10.00 – 12.00

Hound Dog
Marked: USA
$10.00 – 12.00

Mouse and Cheese/Gold
Marked: USA 705
$35.00 – 38.00

Fox and Bag
Marked: Shawnee USA
$60.00 – 65.00

Panda and Cradle
Marked: Shawnee USA 2031
$30.00 – 32.00

Cub Bear and Wagon/Gold
Marked: Shawnee USA 731
$45.00 – 50.00

Pig and Basket
Marked: USA
$8.00 – 10.00

Pig
Marked: USA
$12.00 – 15.00

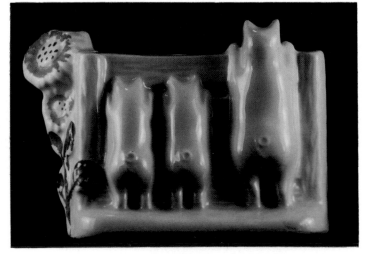

Pig and Wheelbarrow
Marked: USA
$12.00 – 14.00

Three Pigs
Marked: USA
$12.00 – 14.00

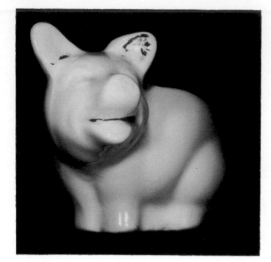

Sitting Pig
No Mark
$8.00 – 10.00

Pig
Marked: USA 760
$12.00 – 15.00

Squirrel and Nut
Marked: USA 713
$30.00 – 35.00

Squirrel and Stump/Gold
Marked: Shawnee 664
$20.00 – 22.00

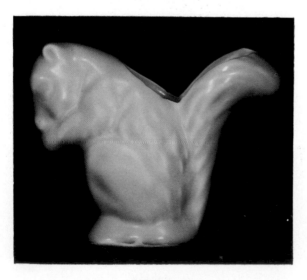

Squirrel
No Mark
$10.00 – 12.00

Squirrel At Stump
Marked: USA
$10.00 – 12.00

Baby Skunk
Marked: Shawnee 512
$30.00 – 35.00

Rabbit with Turnip
Marked: USA 703
$30.00 – 33.00

Rabbit
Marked: USA
$14.00 – 16.00

Rabbit and Stump
Marked: USA 606
$14.00 – 16.00

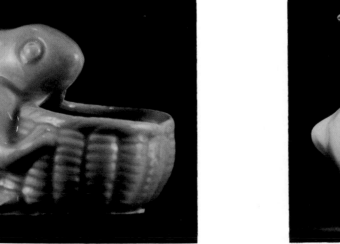

Rabbit and Basket
Marked: USA
$14.00 – 16.00

Rabbit and Cabbage
Marked: USA
$8.00 – 10.00

Frog
Marked: USA
$8.00 – 10.00

Frog and Guitar
Marked: USA
$16.00 – 18.00

Frog on Lily Pad
Marked: USA
$35.00 – 38.00

Turtle/Gold
No Mark
$20.00 – 25.00

Fish Planter or Vase/Gold
Marked: USA 717
$55.00 – 60.00

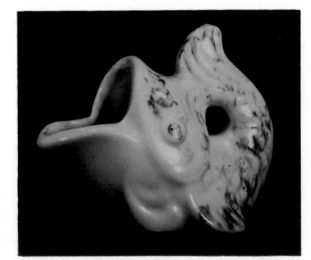

Dolphin
Marked: USA
$10.00 – 12.00

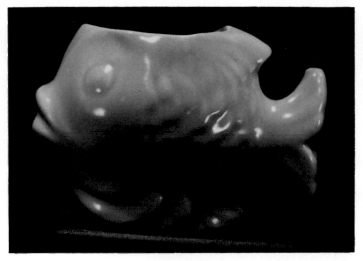

Open Mouth Fish/Gold
Marked: USA 845
$16.00 – 18.00

Blow Fish
Marked: USA
$8.00 – 10.00

Elephant/Gold
Marked: USA 759
$24.00 – 26.00

Elephant
Marked: USA
$18.00 – 20.00

Elephant and Basket
Marked: USA
$18.00 – 20.00

Elephant and Base
Marked: Shawnee USA 501
$55.00 – 65.00

Bull and Base
Marked: Shawnee USA
$55.00 – 65.00

Bull/Gold
Marked: 668
$20.00 – 22.00

Lamb/Gold
Marked: USA 724
$30.00 – 35.00

Dancing Lamb
Marked: USA
$20.00 – 25.00

Circus Pony
Marked: USA
$18.00 – 20.00

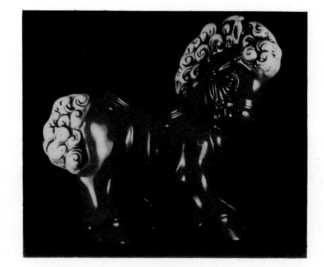

Pony
Marked: Shawnee 506
$35.00 – 40.00

Pony
Marked: Kenwood 1509
$55.00 – 65.00

Circus Horse
Marked: USA
$18.00 – 20.00

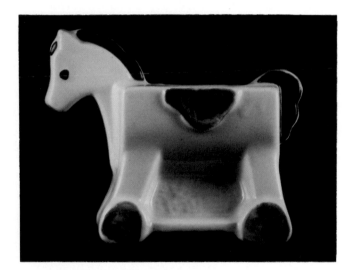

Hobby Horse
Marked: Shawnee 660
$18.00 – 20.00

Rocking Horse
Marked: USA 526
$22.00 – 24.00

Standing Horse
Marked: USA
$12.00 – 15.00

Sitting Pony
Marked: USA
$20.00 – 22.00

Horse
Marked: USA
$10.00 – 12.00

Mexican Cart
Marked: USA 538
$10.00 – 12.00

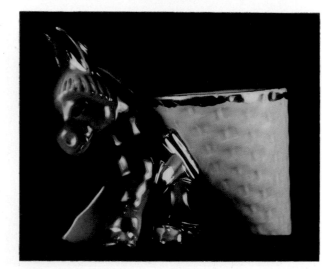

Donkey and Basket/Gold
Marked: USA 671
$30.00 – 35.00

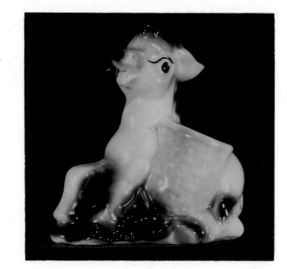

Sitting Donkey and Basket
Marked: Shawnee USA 722
$28.00 – 30.00

Donkey and Cart
Marked: USA
$10.00 – 12.00

Pixie
Marked: USA 536
$8.00 – 10.00

Country Boy at Low Stump/Gold
Marked: USA 532
$22.00 – 24.00

Country Boy at High Stump
Marked: USA 532
$12.00 – 14.00

Boy and Stump
Marked: USA 533
$10.00 – 12.00

Elf and Shoe
Marked: Shawnee 765
$12.00 – 14.00

Boy and Wheelbarrow
Marked: USA 750
$16.00 – 18.00

Boy at Gate
No Mark
$10.00 – 12.00

Girl at Gate
Marked: USA 581
$15.00 – 20.00

Tony the Peddler Rum Carioca
Marked: USA 621
$65.00 – 70.00

Tony the Peddler
Marked: USA 621
$30.00 – 35.00

Girl and Urn
Marked: Shawnee 718
$28.00 – 30.00

Dutch Girl and Sprinkler
Marked: USA
$10.00 – 12.00

Colonial Lady/Gold
Marked: USA 616
$30.00 – 35.00

Girl with Umbrella
Marked: USA 560
$26.00 – 28.00

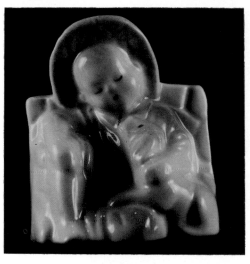

Boy and Dog
Marked: USA 582
$10.00 – 12.00

Southern Girl 6"
Marked: USA
$8.00 – 10.00

Southern Girl with Basket
Marked: USA
$10.00 – 12.00

Southern Girl 8½"
Marked: USA
$10.00 – 12.00

Madonna
Marked: USA
$25.00 – 30.00

Valencia Couple
Marked: USA
$65.00 – 70.00

Girl and Basket
Marked: USA 534
$12.00 – 14.00

Bicycle Built for Two
Marked: Shawnee USA 735
$55.00 – 65.00

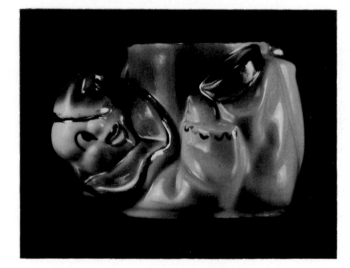

Clown/Gold (Holds 2½" Pot)
Marked: USA 607
$25.00 – 28.00

Children and Shoe
Marked: USA 525
$16.00 – 18.00

Wishing Well/Gold
Marked: Shawnee 710
$25.00 – 28.00

Pixie
No Mark
$12.00 – 15.00

Paper Label on Pixie

Pixie and Wheelbarrow
No Mark
$12.00 – 15.00

Paper Label on
Pixie with Wheelbarrow

Clown with Pot
Marked: USA 619
$12.00 – 15.00

Swan and Elf
Marked: Kenwood 2030
$45.00 – 50.00

Bird on Planting Dish
Marked: Shawnee 767
$25.00 – 30.00

Open Mouth Bird
Marked: USA
$8.00 –10.00

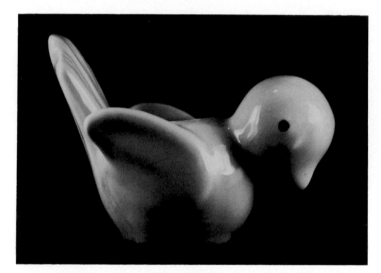

Bird with Head Down
Marked: USA
$8.00 – 10.00

Boy and Chicken
Marked: Shawnee 645
$20.00 – 22.00

Duck and Cart/Gold
Marked: Shawnee 752
$25.00 – 30.00

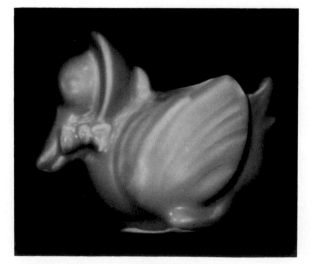

Goose
Marked: USA
$10.00 – 12.00

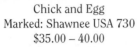

Chick and Egg
Marked: Shawnee USA 730
$35.00 – 40.00

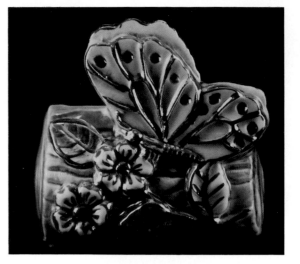

Butterfly/Gold
Marked: Shawnee USA 524
$22.00 – 25.00

Bird and Planter
Marked: USA 502
$10.00 – 15.00

Bird on Shell
Marked: USA
$16.00 – 18.00

Dove and Planting Dish/Gold
Marked: Shawnee 2025
$40.00 – 45.00

Bird
Marked: USA 508
$12.00 – 14.00

Rooster
Marked: Kenwood USA 1503
$30.00 – 35.00

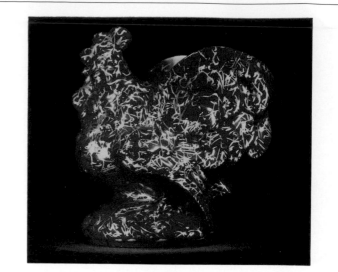

Rooster
Marked: Shawnee USA 503
$30.00 – 35.00

Parakeet
Marked: Shawnee 523
$12.00 – 14.00

Flying Goose
Marked: USA 707
$24.00 – 26.00

Flying Mallard
Marked: Shawnee USA 820
$18.00 – 20.00

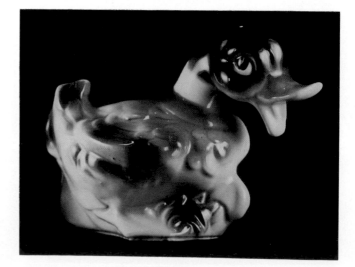

Duckling
Marked: Shawnee USA 720
$24.00 – 26.00

Penguin
Marked: USA
$6.00 – 8.00

Bird on Shell/Tail Up
Marked: USA
$18.00 – 20.00

Birds and Nest
Marked: USA
$16.00 – 18.00

Ducks
Marked: USA
$8.00 – 10.00 Each

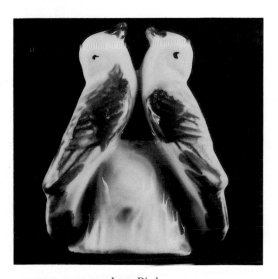

Love Birds
Marked: USA
$10.00 – 12.00

Birds on Driftwood
Marked: Shawnee 502
$45.00 – 50.00

Gazelle Head
Marked: Shawnee 841
$65.00 – 75.00

Fawn and Log
Marked: Shawnee 766
$35.00 – 40.00

Fawn and Stump
Marked: Shawnee 624
$16.00 – 18.00

Zebra and Stump
No Mark
$25.00 – 30.00

Deer and Fawn/Gold
Marked: Shawnee 669
$26.00 – 28.00

Fawn/Gold
Marked: USA 535
$16.00 – 18.00

Deer in Shadow Box/Gold
Marked: Shawnee 850
$30.00 – 35.00

Two Fawns
Marked: Shawnee USA 721
$22.00 – 25.00

Giraffe's Head
Marked: Shawnee USA 841
$60.00 – 65.00

Fawn and Fern
Marked: Shawnee 737
$20.00 – 22.00

Deer
Marked: USA
$8.00 – 10.00

Fawn 6½"
No Mark
$8.00 – 10.00

Fawn 9"
No Mark
$8.00 – 10.00

Lying Deer
Marked: USA
$22.00 – 25.00

Fawn and Stump
No Mark
$16.00 – 18.00

Ram
Marked: Shawnee 515
$20.00 – 25.00

Giraffe
Marked: Shawnee 521
$25.00 – 30.00

Ibex
Marked: USA 613
$10.00 – 12.00

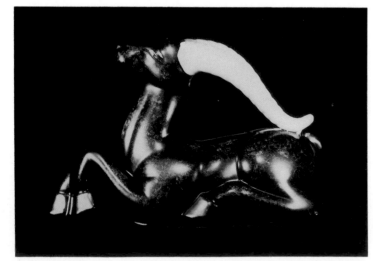

Gazelle Planter/Gold
Marked: USA 614
$75.00 – 80.00

Gazelle on Base 10"
Marked: Shawnee 522 USA
$95.00 – 100.00

High Heel
Marked: USA
$10.00 – 12.00

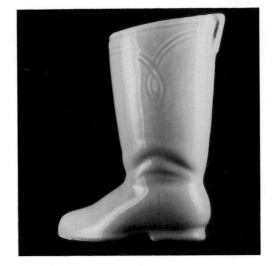

Large Embossed Boot 7"
Marked: USA
$18.00 – 20.00

Elf Shoe/Gold
Marked: Shawnee 765
$18.00 – 20.00

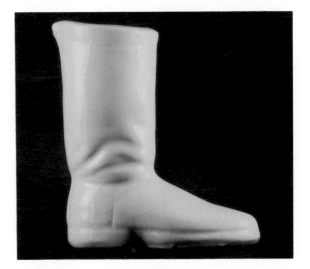

Boot 5"
Marked: Shawnee 734
$8.00 – 10.00

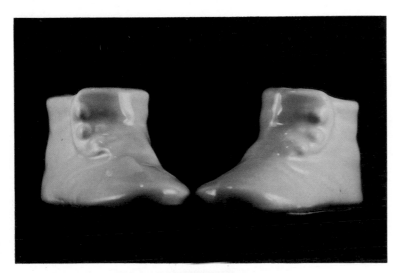

Button Baby Shoe
Marked: USA
Right and Left $10.00 – 12.00 each

Baby Shoe On Base
Marked: USA
$10.00 – 12.00

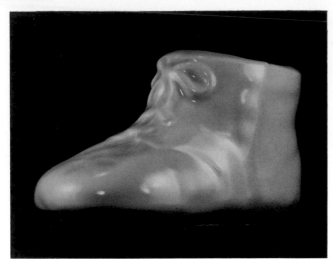

Tie Baby Shoe
Marked: USA
$10.00 – 12.00

Small Embossed Boot 4½"
Marked: USA
$10.00 – 12.00

Sprinkling Can
Embossed Basketweave — Marked: USA
$16.00 – 18.00

Watering Can
Embossed Flower — Marked: USA
$25.00 – 30.00

Coal Bucket
Embossed Flower — Marked: USA
$25.00 – 30.00

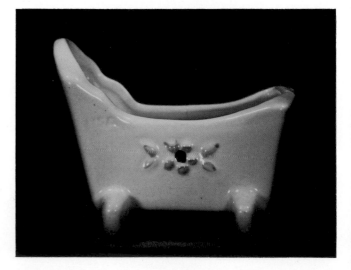

Cradle
Embossed Flower — Marked: USA
$25.00 – 30.00

Coal Stove
Embossed Flower — Marked: USA
$25.00 – 30.00

Baby Bottle
Embossed Flower — Marked: USA
$25.00 – 30.00

Basket
Embossed Flower — Marked: USA 640
$30.00 – 35.00

Basket
Marked: USA
$10.00 – 12.00

Top Hat
Marked: USA
$10.00 – 12.00

Globe/Gold
Marked: Shawnee USA
$50.00 – 55.00

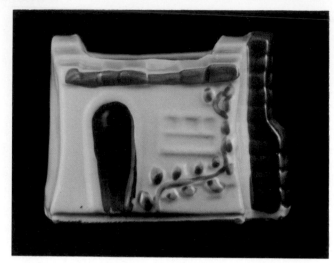

House
Marked: USA J543P
$30.00 – 35.00

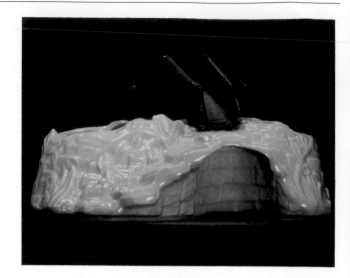

Bridge
Marked: Shawnee USA 756
$18.00 – 20.00

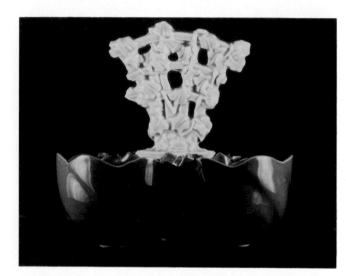

Three Pots and Trellis
Marked: Shawnee 517
$22.00 – 25.00

Double Bow Knot/Gold
Marked: Shawnee 518
$22.00 – 25.00

Flower Pot/Gold
Marked: USA
$12.00 – 14.00

High Chair
Marked: USA 727
$60.00 – 65.00

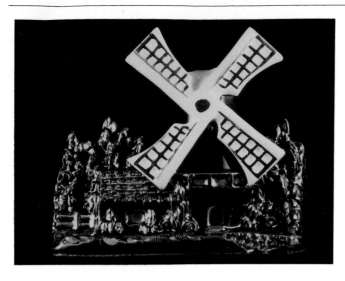

Dutch Mill/Gold
Marked: Shawnee 715
$30.00 – 35.00

Old Mill/Gold
Marked: Shawnee 769
$30.00 – 35.00

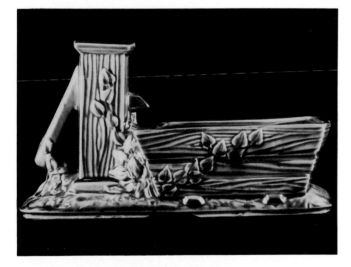

Pump and Trough/Gold
Marked: USA 716
$22.00 – 24.00

Cradle Embossed Lamb/Gold
Marked: Shawnee USA 625
$18.00 – 20.00

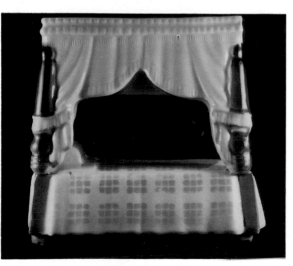

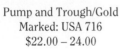

Canopy Bed
Marked: Shawnee 734
$75.00 – 80.00

Shell/Gold
Marked: USA 665
$14.00 – 16.00

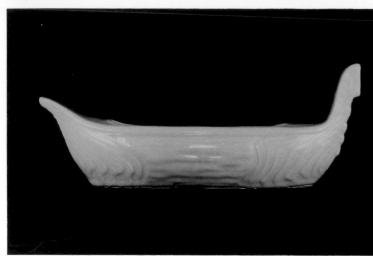

Gondola
Marked: USA
$20.00 – 25.00

Cornucopia
Marked: USA
$8.00 – 10.00

Clock
Marked: USA 1262
$15.00 – 16.00

Piano
Marked: USA 528
$25.00 – 30.00

Polynesian
Marked: Shawnee 896
$40.00 – 45.00

Buddha
Marked: USA 524
$22.00 – 24.00

Girl and Mandolin
Marked: USA 576
$22.00 – 24.00

Chinese Girl
Marked: USA 602
$10.00 – 12.00

Chinese Boy
Marked: USA 601
$10.00 – 12.00

Ancient Chinese Man/Gold
Marked: USA 617
$14.00 – 16.00

Chinese Girl & Urn/Gold
Marked: USA 701
$14.00 – 16.00

Chinese Boy & Vase/Gold
Marked: USA 702
$14.00 – 16.00

Chinese Girl with Book/Gold
Marked: USA 574
$14.00 – 16.00

Chinese Boy & Girl with Mandolin
Marked: USA 573
$12.00 – 14.00

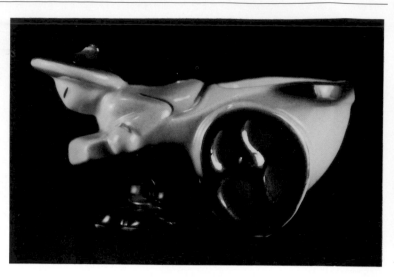

Coolie with Cart/Gold
Marked: USA 539
$14.00 – 16.00

Chinese with Basket
Marked: USA 537
$10.00 – 12.00

Chinese with Cart
Marked: USA
$10.00 – 12.00

Monkey and Stump
No Mark
$30.00 – 35.00

Large Covered Wagon
Marked: Shawnee USA 733
$35.00 – 40.00

Stagecoach
Marked: USA J545P
$30.00 – 35.00

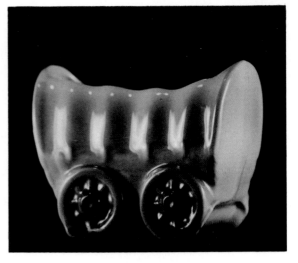

Small Covered Wagon
Marked: USA 514
$8.00 – 10.00

Tractor and Trailer
Marked: Shawnee 680 and 681
$30.00 – 35.00 each

Train Engine
Marked: Shawnee USA
$55.00 – 65.00

Wheelbarrow Embossed
Marked: USA
$20.00 – 22.00

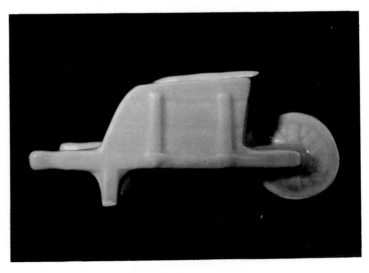

Wheelbarrow
Marked: USA
$8.00 – 10.00

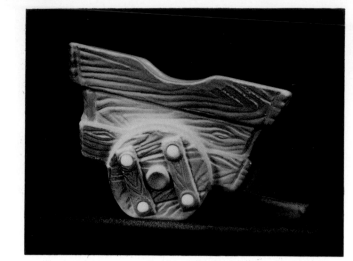

Wheelbarrow – Woodgrain
Marked: USA 775
$8.00 – 10.00

Push Cart
Marked: USA J544P
$30.00 – 35.00

Auto (Eight Spoke) Gold
Marked: USA 506
$22.00 – 24.00

Auto (Four Spoke) Gold
Marked: USA 506
$22.00 – 24.00

Circus Wagon
Marked: USA
$45.00 – 50.00

Caboose
Marked: USA 553
$50.00 – 55.00

The train pieces in solid colors average $25.00 – 30.00 each.

Box Car
Marked: USA 552
$50.00 – 55.00

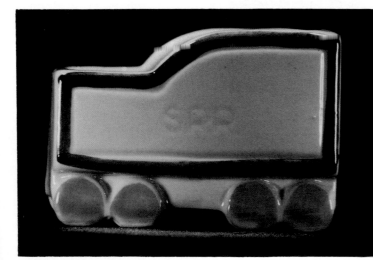

Coal Car
Marked: USA 551
$50.00 – 55.00

Train Engine
Marked: USA 550
$50.00 – 55.00

FIGURINES

Scotty 7¹/₂"
Marked: USA
$25.00 – 30.00

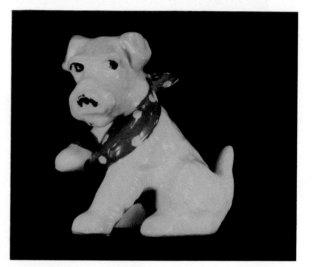

Scotty with Sling 5¹/₄"
No Mark
$25.00 – 30.00

Muggsy/Gold 5¹/₂"
Marked: USA
$80.00 – 85.00

Dog 6½"
No Mark
$25.00 – 30.00

Lamb 6½"
No Mark
$25.00 – 30.00

Donkey 6½"
No Mark
$10.00 – 12.00

Gazelle/Gold 5"
Marked: USA 614
$80.00 – 85.00

SMALL FIGURINES

The small figurines designed in the late 1930's were also referred to by Shawnee as small ornaments and flower bowl inserts. They were all available in Bright White, Flax Blue, Old Ivory, Turquoise, and Dusty Rose. All of the small figurines shown, except the Southern girl, were dropped from production in 1942.

Southern Girl 4½"
Marked: USA
$18.00 – 20.00

Crane 5¼"
No Mark
$16.00 – 18.00

Crane 5¼"
No Mark
$16.00 – 18.00

Doe 4½"
No Mark
$16.00 – 18.00

Fawn 4½"
No Mark
$16.00 – 18.00

Deer 4½"
No Mark
$16.00 – 18.00

LORRAINE WARE

Lorraine was available in six colors: Matt Eggshell White, Vellum Powder Blue, Burgundy, Old English Ivory, Jonquil Yellow, and Turquoise. Each piece could be obtained in any of the six colors.

The vases were designed with large flaring tops, and the jardinieres were made so standard flower pots would fit inside. The miniatures were designed to display small bouquets.

Some Lorraine Ware pieces are found throughout the book in their appropriate sections.

VASES

Shawnee manufactured vases from the day they opened until the day the factory doors were closed. In some cases the same vase would be produced in several sizes and in as many as six to eight different colors. In order to picture as many different vases as possible, we chose not to duplicate the same vase in all of its color variations. However, we have tried to show an example of the numerous colors that Shawnee used over the years.

Cornucopia 3½"
Marked: USA
$12.00 – 14.00

LEFT: Many of these vases were made but not for production. They were used only in the lab for the testing of new glazes. If a glaze was applied and did not meet Shawnee standards, the vase was destroyed. If it was decided that the new glaze would be used for production, it would be made in a large quantity, and the original test piece would eventually be destroyed.

Glaze Test Piece
Marked WCH 1937

Wheat 3½"
Marked: USA 1208
$16.00 – 18.00

Embossed Flower/Gold 3½"
Marked: USA
$22.00 – 24.00

Fan 4"
Marked: USA 1264
$14.00 – 16.00

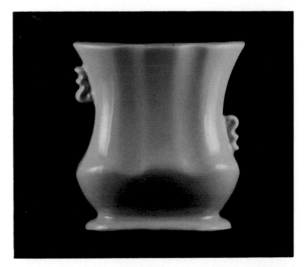

Double 4½"
Marked: USA
$10.00 – 12.00

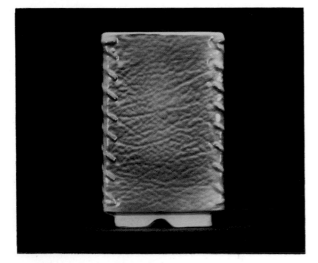

Burlap 4"
Marked: USA
$10.00 – 12.00

Ribbed 5"
Marked: USA
$10.00 – 12.00

Embossed Cornucopia 5"
Marked: USA
$12.00 – 14.00

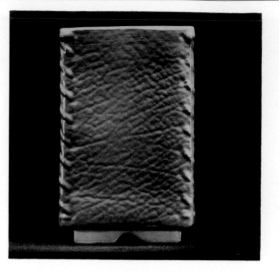

Burlap 5"
Marked: USA 885
$10.00 – 12.00

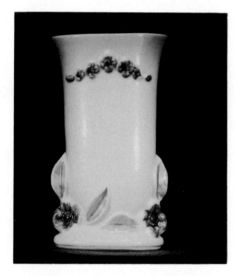

Embossed Flowers 5"
Marked: USA 1268
$22.00 – 24.00

Bud Vase 5"
Marked: USA
$12.00 – 14.00

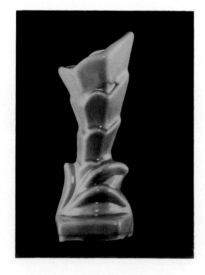

Bud Vase 5"
Marked: USA 705
$12.00 – 14.00

Bud Vase/Gold 5"
Marked: USA 1125
$14.00 – 16.00

Bud Vase 5"
Marked: USA 1135
$12.00 – 14.00

Embossed Flowers 5"
Marked: USA 1205
$22.00 – 24.00

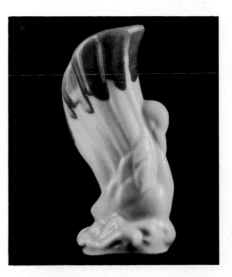

Wheat/Gold 5"
Marked: USA
$20.00 – 22.00

Swan Bud Vase 5"
Marked: USA 725
$10.00 – 12.00

Embossed 5"
Marked: USA
$10.00 – 12.00

Double 5"
Marked: Shawnee USA
$16.00 – 18.00

Conventional 5"
Marked: USA
$10.00 – 12.00

Bud Vase/Gold 5"
Marked: USA 1115
$14.00 – 16.00

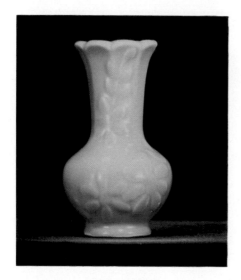

Embossed 5"
Marked: USA
$12.00 – 14.00

Conventional 5"
Marked: USA
$8.00 – 10.00

Embossed Double Handle 5"
Marked: USA
$10.00 – 12.00

Cornucopia/Gold 5"
Marked: USA 835
$14.00 – 16.00

Cornucopia 5"
Marked: USA
$14.00 – 16.00

Cornucopia 5"
Marked: Shawnee USA 865
$14.00 – 16.00

Cornucopia Girl and Boy 5"
Marked: USA 1275 and USA 1265
$12.00 – 14.00 each

Embossed Flowers 5"
Marked: USA
$20.00 – 22.00

Embossed/Gold 5"
Marked: USA 1225
$24.00 – 26.00

Geometric 5"
Marked: USA
$12.00 – 14.00

Swirl 5"
Marked: USA
$12.00 – 14.00

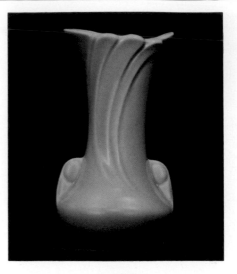

Swirl 5"
Marked: USA
$12.00 – 14.00

Butterfly Bud/Gold 5¹/₂"
Marked: USA 735
$12.00 – 14.00

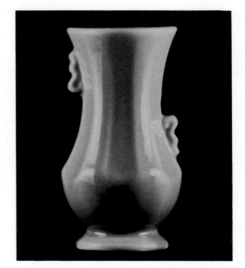

Double Handle 5¹/₂"
Marked: USA
$10.00 – 12.00

Swirl 5¹/₂"
Marked: USA
$12.00 – 14.00

Rope Handle 5¹/₂"
Marked: USA
$12.00 – 14.00

Tulip 5½"
Marked: USA
$12.00 – 14.00

Urn 5½"
Marked: USA
$10.00 – 12.00

Embossed Flowers 5½"
Marked: USA
$14.00 – 16.00

Flared 5½"
Marked: USA
$10.00 – 12.00

Embossed Iris 5½"
Marked: USA
$14.00 – 16.00

Embossed Cornucopia 5½"
Marked: USA
$12.00 – 14.00

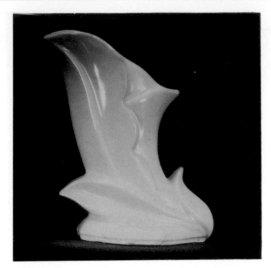

Cornucopia Leaf 5½"
Marked: Shawnee USA
$12.00 – 14.00

Ribbed 5½"
Marked: USA
$18.00 – 20.00

Cornucopia 6"
Marked: USA
$16.00 – 18.00

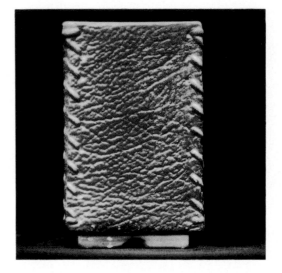

Burlap 6"
Marked: USA 885
$10.00 – 12.00

Embossed Iris 6"
Marked: USA
$16.00 – 18.00

Swan/Gold 6"
Marked: USA 806
$24.00 – 26.00

Cornucopia 6"
Marked: USA 210
$12.00 – 14.00

Butterfly 6"
Marked: USA 680
$14.00 – 16.00

Embossed 6"
Marked: USA
$8.00 – 10.00

Wheat Cornucopia/Gold 6"
Marked: USA 1256
$20.00 – 22.00

Wheat 6"
Marked: USA 1266
$20.00 – 22.00

Experimental Vase 6"
Marked: Shawnee USA 1409
$38.00 – 40.00

Bottom of experimental piece

Cornucopia 6"
Marked: USA
$12.00 – 14.00

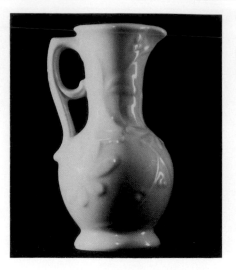

Embossed Pitcher 6½"
Marked: USA
$12.00 – 14.00

Embossed 6½"
Marked: USA
$16.00 – 18.00

Cornucopia 6½"
Marked: USA
$12.00 – 14.00

Basketweave 6½"
Marked: Shawnee 842
$10.00 – 12.00

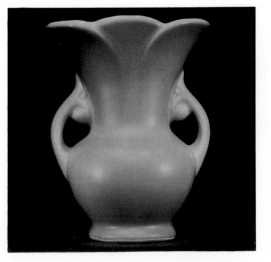

Conventional 6½"
Marked: USA
$10.00 – 12.00

Embossed Cornucopia 6½"
Marked: USA
$16.00 – 18.00

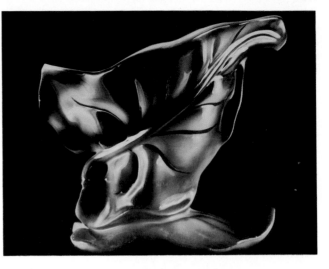

Leaf/Gold 6½"
Marked: USA 822
$35.00 – 40.00

Dolphin Pitcher/Gold 6½"
Marked: Shawnee 828
$40.00 – 45.00

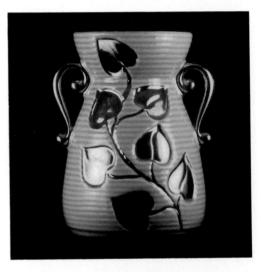

Embossed Philodendron/Gold 6½"
Marked: Shawnee 805
$35.00 – 40.00

Leaf/Gold 7"
Marked: USA 821
$22.00 – 24.00

Embossed Flower 7"
Marked: USA 1257
$22.00 – 24.00

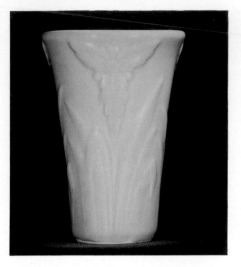

Embossed Flower & Leaf 7"
Marked: USA
$20.00 – 22.00

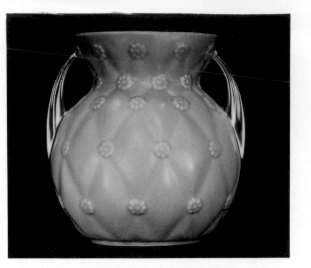

Embossed Flower & Diamond/Gold 7"
Marked: Shawnee 827
$26.00 – 28.00

Conventional 7"
Marked: USA 554
$10.00 – 12.00

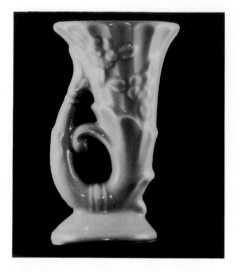

Embossed 7"
Marked: USA
$14.00 – 16.00

Ribbed & Embossed Flowers 7"
Marked: USA
$16.00 – 18.00

Embossed 7"
Marked: USA
$10.00 – 12.00

Wheat/Gold 7"
Marked: USA 1267
$26.00 – 28.00

Hand 7"
Marked: USA
$12.00 – 14.00

Basketweave 7"
Marked: Shawnee USA 842
$12.00 – 14.00

Conventional 7"
Marked: USA
$10.00 – 12.00

Ribbed 7½"
Marked: USA
$10.00 – 12.00

Embossed 7½"
Marked: USA
$12.00 – 14.00

Wheat 8"
Marked: USA 1258
$16.00 – 18.00

Flared with Double Handle 8"
Marked: USA
$12.00 – 14.00

Flared 8"
Marked: Shawnee USA 838
$12.00 – 14.00

Conventional 8"
Marked: USA 2012
$14.00 – 16.00

Bud Vase/Gold and Decals 8"
Marked: USA 1168
$22.00 – 24.00

Bud Vase/Gold 8"
Marked: USA 878
$20.00 – 22.00

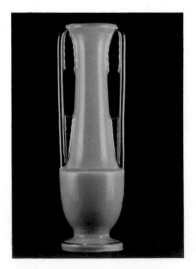

Bud Vase/Gold 8"
Marked: USA 1178
$20.00 – 22.00

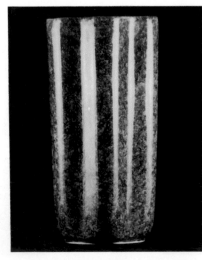

Rolled 8"
Marked: USA 2011
$14.00 – 16.00

Embossed 8"
Marked: USA 592
$12.00 – 14.00

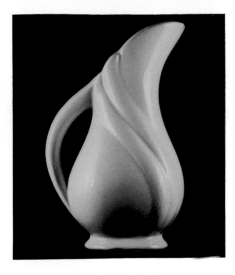

Swirl Pitcher 8"
Marked: USA
$10.00 – 12.00

Moor Head Girl/Gold 8"
No Mark, Has Glazed Bottom
$50.00 – 55.00

Moor Head Boy/Gold 8"
No Mark, Has Glazed Bottom
$50.00 – 55.00

Ribbed Pitcher/Gold 8"
Marked: USA
$26.00 – 28.00

Hand 8"
Marked: USA
$16.00 – 18.00

Geometric 8"
Marked: USA 808
$16.00 – 18.00

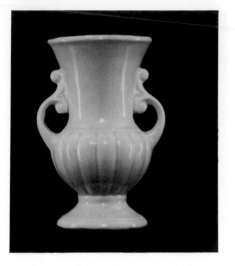

Conventional 8"
Marked: USA
$12.00 – 14.00

Flared 8¹/₂"
Marked: USA
$12.00 – 14.00

Embossed 8¹/₂"
Marked: USA
$12.00 – 14.00

Ribbed 8¹/₂"
Marked: Shawnee USA
$14.00 – 16.00

Fluted 8¹/₂"
Marked: Shawnee USA 3009
$16.00 – 18.00

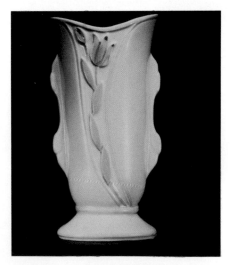

Embossed 8¹/₂"
Marked: USA 1269
$35.00 – 38.00

Burlap 9"
Marked: USA 879
$14.00 – 16.00

Scalloped 9"
Marked: Shawnee USA
$14.00 – 16.00

Wheat 9"
Marked: USA 1259
$24.00 – 26.00

Leaf/Gold 9"
Marked: Shawnee 823
$40.00 – 45.00

Ribbed Pitcher 9"
Marked: USA
$12.00 – 14.00

Dove 9"
Marked: USA 829
$16.00 – 18.00

Bow Knot/Gold 9"
Marked: USA 819
$26.00 – 28.00

Geometric 9"
Marked: USA
$18.00 – 20.00

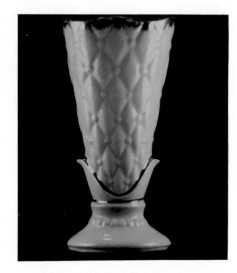

Pineapple/Gold 9"
Marked: Shawnee 839
$22.00 – 24.00

Hand 9½"
Marked: USA
$18.00 – 20.00

Burlap 9½"
Marked: USA 880
$16.00 – 18.00

Embossed Cornucopia 10"
Marked: USA
$16.00 – 18.00

Flared 10"
Marked: Shawnee USA
$18.00 – 20.00

Conventional 10"
Marked: USA 2013
$20.00 – 22.00

Bulbous 10"
Marked: Kenwood USA 2014
$22.00 – 25.00

Swirl 10"
Marked: USA 416
$22.00 – 24.00

Bulbous 10"
Marked: Kenwood USA 1515
$22.00 – 25.00

Bulbous 10"
Marked: Shawnee USA 890
$22.00 – 25.00

Swirl 10"
Marked: USA
$20.00 – 22.00

Double Handled 10"
Marked: USA
$20.00 – 22.00

Stem Vase 10½"
Marked: Shawnee USA 1816
$22.00 – 24.00

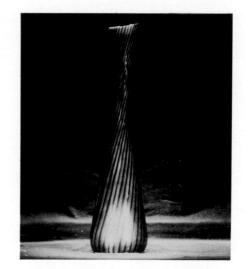

Stem Vase 10½"
Marked: Shawnee USA 1402; Unglazed Bottom
$22.00 – 24.00

Oriental 12"
No Mark, Has Paper Label
$22.00 – 24.00

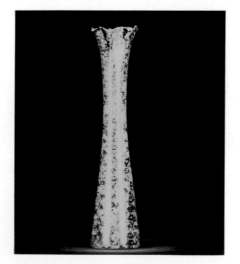

Stem Vase 12"
Marked: Shawnee USA 2116
$20.00 – 22.00

POT AND SAUCERS

The African Violet Pot and Saucers were offered in Pastel Pink, Citrus Yellow, or White all with Tropical Green Saucers. They were available in 3", 5", and 6½".

3"
Shawnee USA 533
$10.00 – $12.00

5"
Shawnee USA 534
$10.00 – 12.00

6½"
Shawnee USA 535
$12.00 – 14.00

The Duotone Pot and Saucers were available in 4", 5", and 6". They were given this name because of the two-tone color combinations of Yellow and Black, Turquoise and White, and Pink and Green.

4"
Shawnee USA 484
$10.00 – 12.00

5"
Shawnee USA 485
$10.00 – 12.00

6"
Shawnee USA 486
$12.00 – 14.00

These pot and saucers are embossed with small flowers or diamonds with small flowers on both the flower pot and the saucer. Available in 3", 4", 4⅝", 5", and 6" in assorted colors of Green, Burgundy, Yellow, Hunter Green, and Royal Blue.

3"
Shawnee USA 454
$10.00 – 12.00

5"
Shawnee USA 455
$10.00 – 12.00

6"
Shawnee USA 456
$10.00 – 12.00

The Bow Knot Pot and Saucers sizes are 3½", 4½", 5½", and 6½" in Turquoise, Powder Blue, Eggshell White, Burgundy, Old English Ivory, and Jonquil Yellow.

Bow Knot 4½"
Marked: USA
$10.00 – 12.00

Bow Knot 5½"
Marked: USA
$10.00 – 12.00

Leaf Embossed 5"
Marked: Shawnee USA 465
Hunter Green, Yellow, and Chartreuse
$14.00 – 16.00

The Flared African Violet Pot and Saucers were offered in Lime, Bermuda Green, and Velvet Pink with a Tiara glaze. The sizes available are 3", 5", 6¼".

The Ribbed Duotone Pot and Saucers were offered in Turquoise, Citrus Yellow, or Pastel Pink with White saucers. The sizes available are 4", 5", and 6".

Flared African Violet 3"
Marked: Shawnee USA 533
$12.00 – 14.00

Flared African Violet 5"
Marked: Shawnee USA 534
$12.00 – 15.00

Ribbed Duotone 4"
Marked: USA 494
$10.00 – 12.00

Textured 4"
Marked: Shawnee USA
$10.00 – 12.00

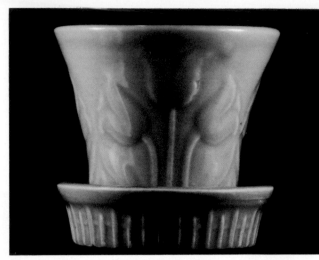

Tulip Embossed 4¹/₂"
Marked: USA
$10.00 – 12.00

Flared Petals 5"
Marked: Shawnee USA 466
$16.00 – 18.00

Embossed Swirl 3¹/₂"
Marked: USA
$10.00 – 12.00

Embossed Flower 3¹/₂"
Marked: USA
$10.00 – 12.00

Geometric Design 2¹/₂"
Marked: USA
$10.00 –12.00

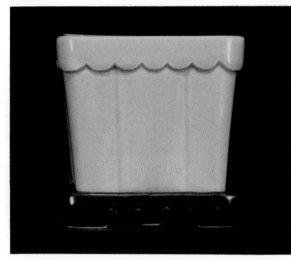

Duotone Square
Marked: Shawnee USA 410
$10.00 – 12.00

Test Piece
Pot, no saucer
$40.00 – 45.00

Bottom of Test Piece
Marked: Shawnee USA 443
M-9 5697

Test Piece
Pot, no saucer
$40.00 – 45.00

Bottom of Test Piece
Marked: N - Plat Shawnee
USA 443

JARDINIERES

A Jardiniere is an ornamental stand for plants. We normally think of a jardiniere as being a large container. However, Shawnee made and labeled pots as small as 2½" a jardiniere. Most of the round jardinieres were made to fit companion size red clay pots and were advertised as such.

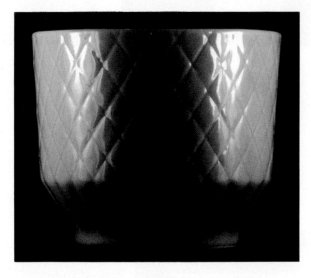

Criss Cross 5½". Also available in 4½" & 6½".
Marked: Shawnee USA 456
Forest Green, Tropical Green and Golden Yellow
$10.00 – 12.00

Classic 5½". Also available in 6½".
Marked: Shawnee USA 456
Forest Green, Pumpkin, and Cornflower
with a Tiara glaze.
$10.00 – 12.00

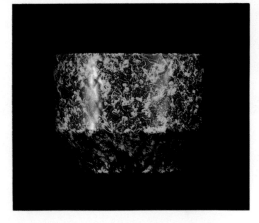

Classic 4½"
Marked: Shawnee USA 455
Forest Green, Pumpkin, and Cornflower
with a Tiara glaze.
$10.00 – 12.00

The following jardinieres have been verified through Shawnee literature. We have given the sizes and have shown as many of the various colors as possible.

2"
Marked: USA
$8.00 – 10.00

2¹/₂"
Marked: USA
$8.00 – 10.00

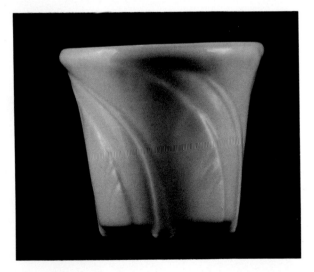

2¹/₂"
Marked: USA
$8.00 – 10.00

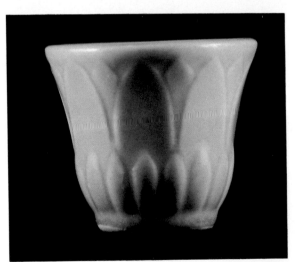

2¹/₂"
Marked: USA
$8.00 – 10.00

3"
Marked: USA
$8.00 – 10.00

3¹/₂"
Marked: USA
$8.00 – 10.00

3¹/₂"
Marked: USA
$8.00 – 10.00

3¹/₂"
Marked: USA
$8.00 – 10.00

3¹/₂"
Marked: USA
$10.00 – 12.00

3¹/₂"
Marked: USA
$10.00 – 12.00

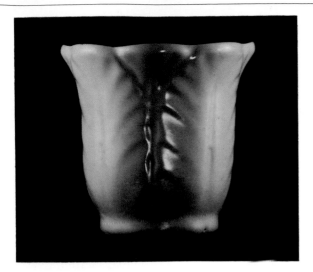

3½"
Marked: USA
$8.00 – 10.00

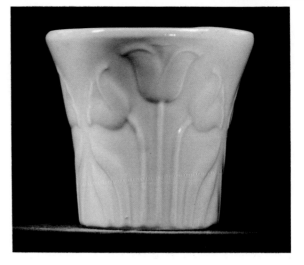

5"
Marked: USA
$8.00 – 10.00

5"
Marked: USA
$8.00 – 10.00

5½"
Marked: USA 436
$10.00 – 12.00

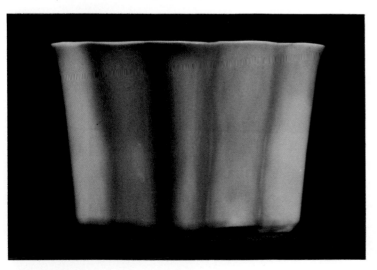

5½"
Marked: USA 405
$10.00 – 12.00

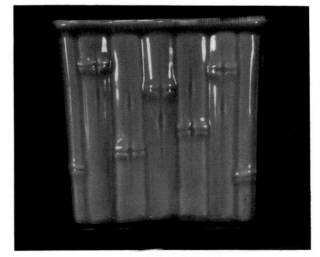

5"
Marked: USA 4055
$10.00 – 12.00

FLOWER BOWLS/
CONSOLE BOWLS

The flower bowls below came in colors of Matte White, Old Ivory, Flax Blue, Turquoise, Yellow, Dark Blue, Dark Green, and Burgundy. The dark colors indicate the earlier production. When the flower bowls were sold in a set with matching candle holders, they were called console bowls.

Conventional Design 8" Round
Marked: USA
$25.00 – 35.00

Leaf Embossed 8¼" Round
Marked: USA
$25.00 – 35.00

Scalloped Embossed 8" Round
Marked: USA
$25.00 – 35.00

Flared 10" Round
Marked: Shawnee USA
White/Gold, Black/Gold
$25.00 – 35.00

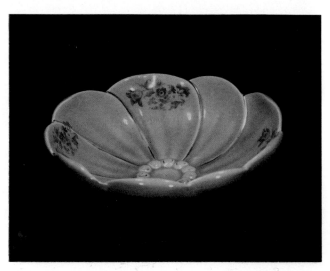

Magnolia Blossom/Gold 9" Round
Marked: USA
White, Turquoise, Old Ivory, Dusty Rose,
Gold Trimmed $70.00 – 75.00; no gold $35.00 – 40.00

Wheat Design 9½" x 6" Oval
Marked: USA
Flax Blue, Dusty Rose, Turquoise, Old Ivory, White
$22.00 – 24.00

Four Fluted Cornucopias 10½" x 6" Oval
No Mark
Flax Blue, Dusty Rose, Turquoise, Old Ivory, White
$18.00 – 20.00

Scalloped 5½" Round
Marked: USA
$12.00 – 14.00

Ribbed 10" x 4" Oval
Marked: USA
Flax Blue, Dusty Rose, Turquoise, Old Ivory, White
$18.00 – 20.00

Flower Bowl/Gold
Stamped: Shaffer 24K Gold
Marked: USA 1501
$20.00 – 25.00

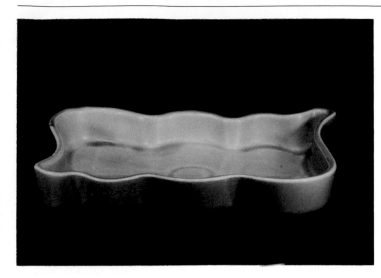

Low Flower Bowl 8" Rectangular
Marked: USA 3003; Multi-Color
$10.00 – 12.00

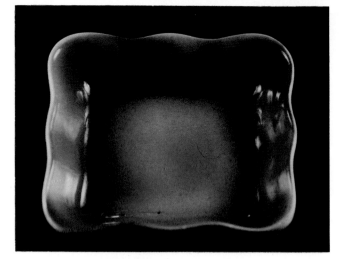

Bon Bon Dish 5" Rectangular
Marked: USA 352; Multi-Color
$8.00 – 10.00

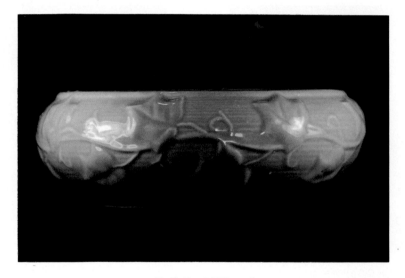
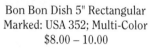

Bulb Bowl 8" Round
Marked: Shawnee USA 3025; Yellow and Green
$8.00 – 10.00

Flower Bowl/Decorated
Painted under Glaze
$40.00 – 45.00

Bottom of Decorated Flower Bowl
Marked: Shawnee USA

CANDLE HOLDERS

Most of the candleholders shown were made to match flower bowls. The candle holders were packaged two dozen to a carton, and prices ranged from $2.28 per dozen to $4.00 per dozen for the Magnolia Blossom. The Conventional design and the Magnolia Blossom were dropped from production in October 1942. The Four Fluted Cornucopias and the Leaf Embossed were introduced in 1943. The sizes indicated are the height.

Conventional Design 3¼"
Marked: USA; Matt White, Old Ivory, Flax Blue, Turquoise,
Yellow, Dark Blue, Dark Green, and Burgundy
$22.00 – 24.00 a pair

Leaf Embossed 3¼"
Marked: USA; Matt White, Old Ivory, Flax Blue, Turquoise,
Yellow, Dark Blue, Dark Green, and Burgundy
$22.00 – 24.00 a pair

Single Cornucopia 3½"
Marked: USA; Matt White, Old Ivory, Flax Blue, Turquoise,
Yellow, Dark Blue, Dark Green, and Burgundy
$15.00 – 18.00 a pair

Four Fluted Cornucopias 4"
No Mark; Matt White, Old Ivory, Flax Blue, Turquoise,
Yellow, Dark Blue, Dark Green, and Burgundy
$18.00 – 20.00 a pair

Open Cornucopias 4"
Marked: USA; Bright White, Yellow
$6.00 – 8.00 a pair

Traditional in Gold 3"
Marked: Shawnee 3026; Burnt Orange, Green
$35.00 – 40.00 single

Traditional in Platinum 3"
Marked: Shawnee USA 3026; Burnt Orange, Green
$40.00 – 45.00 single

Marked: Flared 2"
Shawnee USA; White/Gold, Black/Gold
$26.00 – 28.00 a pair

Magnolia Blossom/Gold 3"
Marked: USA
White, Flax Blue, Old Ivory, Dusty Rose
$30.00 – 35.00 a pair in gold

Modern 6½"
No Mark,
White/Gold, Black/Gold
$26.00 – 28.00 a pair

Aladdin 2¼"
Marked: USA
White, Turquoise, Yellow, Flax Blue
$10.00 – 12.00 single

93

FLOWER FROGS

What we normally refer to as Flower Frogs were called Flower Bowl Inserts by Shawnee. We have verified them in colors of Turquoise, Powder Blue, Eggshell White, Burgundy, Old English Ivory, and Jonquil Yellow.

Flower Bouquet 4¹/₂"
Paper Label
$40.00 – 45.00

Snail 4x5"
Marked: USA
$40.00 – 45.00

Turtle 4x5"
No Mark
$40.00 – 45.00

Sea Horse 3¹/₂"
No Mark
$40.00 – 45.00

Dolphin – Low Base 3¹/₂"
No Mark
$40.00 – 45.00

Dolphin – High Base 4¹/₄"
No Mark
$40.00 – 45.00

Swan – High Base 4¹/₄"
No Mark
$40.00 – 45.00

The Seahorse, Dolphin, and Swan are available on high and low bases.

HANGING BASKETS

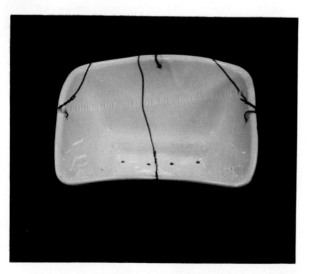

8"
Marked: Shawnee USA 450
$65.00 – 70.00

3"
Marked: USA 685
$55.00 – 60.00

PLANTING DISHES

14¹/₂"
Marked: Shawnee USA 2002
$18.00 – 20.00

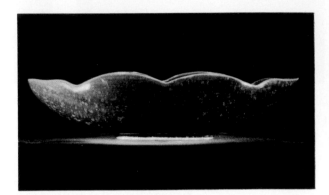

14¹/₂"
Marked: Kenwood USA 2002
$18.00 – 20.00

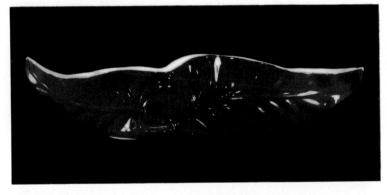

14¹/₂"
Marked: Shawnee USA 441
$18.00 – 20.00

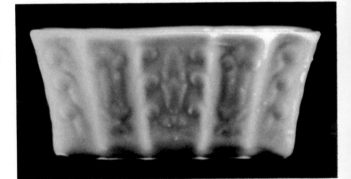

5"
Marked: USA
$8.00 – 10.00

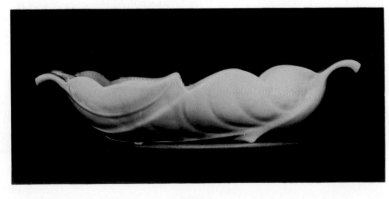

14¹/₂"
Marked: Shawnee USA 442
$18.00 – 20.00

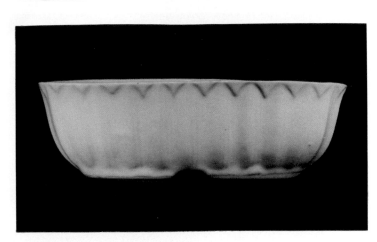

6½"
Marked: Shawnee USA
$6.00 – 8.00

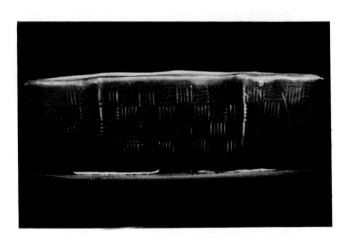

9½"
Marked: USA 150
$6.00 – 8.00

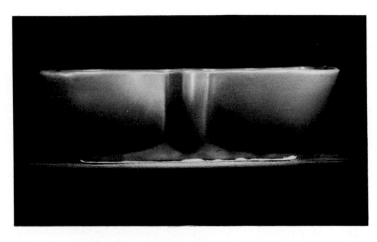

8¼"
Marked: USA 151
$6.00 – 8.00

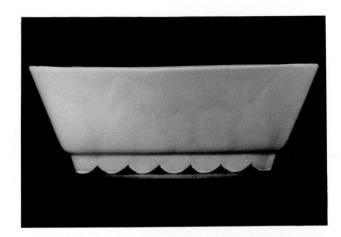

9"
Marked: USA 163
$6.00 – 8.00

6½"
Marked: USA
$8.00 – 10.00

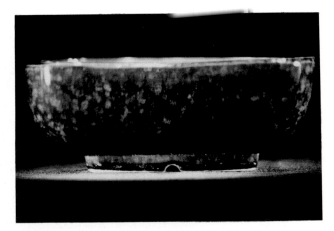

7"
Marked: Shawnee USA 2004
$8.00 – 10.00

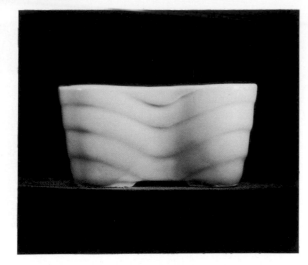

5"
Marked: USA
$6.00 – 8.00

6"
Marked: Shawnee USA 154
$8.00 – 10.00

7½"
Marked: USA 1803
$8.00 – 10.00

6"
Marked: USA 520
$14.00 – 16.00

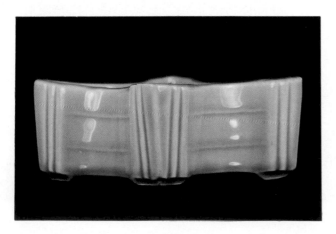

4"
Marked: USA
$6.00 – 8.00

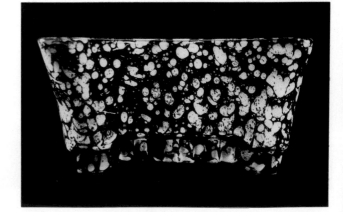

6"
Marked: USA 1001
$6.00 – 8.00

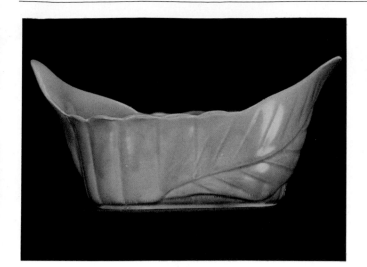

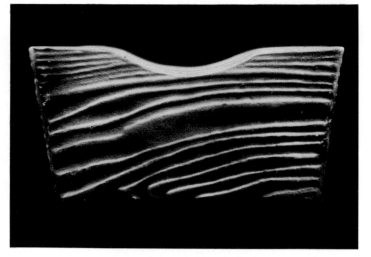

8¹/₂"
Marked: Shawnee USA 439
$14.00 – 16.00

5¹/₂"
Marked: Shawnee USA 400
$10.00 – 12.00

6¹/₂"
Marked: USA
$6.00 – 8.00

6¹/₂"
Marked: USA 182
$12.00 – 14.00

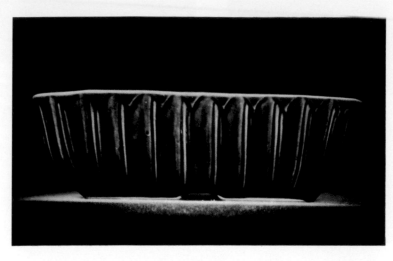

8"
Marked: Shawnee USA 160
$8.00 – 10.00

9½"
Marked: USA 152
$10.00 – 12.00

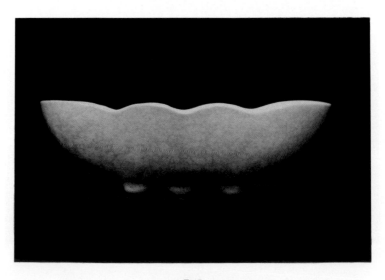

7½"
Marked: USA 1005
$10.00 – 12.00

WALL POCKETS

The Scotty Dog wall pocket was the first decorative piece designed by Louise Bauer in 1937. It is 9" high and 5" across in Blue, Green, Burgundy, Yellow, and White.

Scotty Dog
No Mark
$65.00 – 70.00

Little Jack Horner
Marked: USA 585
$35.00 – 40.00

Little Bo Peep
Marked: USA 586
$35.00 – 40.00

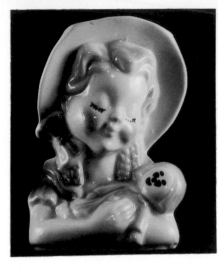

Girl's Head
Marked: USA 810
$35.00 – 40.00

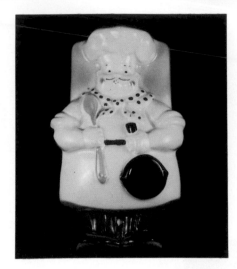

Chef
Marked: USA
$38.00 – 42.00

Grandfather Clock/Gold
Marked: USA 1261
$45.00 – 50.00

Clock/Gold
Marked: USA 530
$35.00 – 40.00

Telephone/Gold
Marked: USA 529
$55.00 – 60.00

Bow/Gold
Marked: USA 434
$30.00 – 35.00

Cornucopia with Bird
No Mark
$20.00 – 25.00

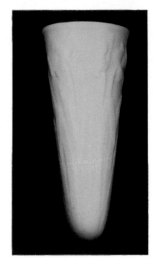

Birds on Roof
Marked: USA
$30.00 – 35.00

Bird House/Gold
Marked: USA 830
$30.00 – 35.00

Embossed Daffodil
No Mark
$30.00 – 35.00

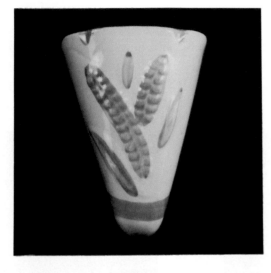

Wheat
No Mark
$30.00 – 35.00

Red Feather
No Mark
$40.00 – 45.00

Star
Marked: USA
$30.00 – 35.00

Flower
Marked: USA 433
$30.00 – 35.00

MINIATURES

Miniatures have become very collectible. They are usually inexpensive and do not require much space to display. Shawnee Pottery miniatures went into production in 1937 and were continued through the late 1940's. They were advertised as having multiple uses. We have found them listed under small ornaments, flower bowl inserts, aquarium ornaments, and animal ornaments. Other than shelf pieces, they were also given as party favors, premiums, and souvenirs. Most of them have been found in at least four different colors and sometimes as many as six. On the animal miniatures the eyes, ears, nose, and feet were all decorated with cold paint. Unfortunately, the cold paint is worn on most of the pieces found today. Initially, the miniatures could be purchased in assortment packs of nine dozen, consisting of one dozen of each kind. The price of the assortment pack was $1.87 per dozen. The colors offered were: Matt White, Bright White, Old Ivory, Flax Blue, Turquoise, Dusty Rose, Dark Blue, Dark Green, Burgundy, and Yellow. The sizes of the miniatures range from ¾" to 3¼".

Vase/Gold Gilded
Marked: USA
$25.00 – 30.00

Vase
Marked: USA
$18.00 – 20.00

Vase
Marked: USA
$18.00 – 20.00

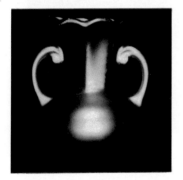

Vase
Marked: USA
$18.00 – 20.00

Vase
Marked: USA
$18.00 – 20.00

Vase
Marked: USA
$18.00 – 20.00

Vase
Marked: USA
$18.00 – 20.00

Vase
Marked: USA
$18.00 – 20.00

Vase
Marked: USA
$18.00 – 20.00

Vase
Marked: USA
$18.00 – 20.00

Vase
Marked: USA
$18.00 – 20.00

Vase
Marked: USA
$18.00 – 20.00

Vase
Marked: USA
$18.00 – 20.00

Vase
Marked: USA
$18.00 – 20.00

Vase
Marked: USA
$18.00 – 20.00

Vase
Marked: USA
$18.00 – 20.00

Vase
No Mark,
Experimental Piece, Glazed with
leftover A E Tile glaze in 1937
$45.00 – 50.00

Pitcher
Marked: USA
$18.00 – 20.00

Pitcher
Marked: USA
$18.00 – 20.00

Pitcher
Marked: USA
$18.00 – 20.00

Pitcher
Marked: USA
$18.00 – 20.00

Pitcher
Marked: USA
$18.00 – 20.00

Pitcher
Marked: USA
$18.00 – 20.00

Pitcher
Marked: USA
$18.00 – 20.00

Cornucopia
Marked: USA
$22.00 – 24.00

Cornucopia
Marked: USA
$18.00 – 20.00

Cornucopia
Marked: USA
$18.00 – 20.00

Cornucopia
Marked: USA
$18.00 – 20.00

Pitcher
Marked: USA
$18.00 – 20.00

Planter
Marked: USA
$18.00 – 20.00

Planter
Marked: USA
$20.00 – 22.00

Planter
Marked: USA
$20.00 – 22.00

Hand Vase
Marked: USA
$24.00 – 26.00

Swan Vase
Marked: USA
$18.00 – 20.00

Swan Vase
Marked: USA
$18.00 – 20.00

Leaf Vase
Marked: USA
$18.00 – 20.00

Embossed Basket
Marked: USA
$24.00 – 26.00

Basketweave Basket
Marked: USA
$24.00 – 26.00

Watering Can
Marked: USA
$24.00 – 26.00

Sprinkling Can
Marked: USA
$24.00 – 26.00

Watering Can
Marked: USA
$24.00 – 26.00

Baby Buggy
Marked: USA
$18.00 – 20.00

Vase
Marked: USA
$18.00 – 20.00

Vase
Marked: USA
$24.00 – 26.00

Vase
Marked: USA
$18.00 – 20.00

Vase
Marked: USA
$20.00 – 22.00

Vase
Marked: USA
$24.00 – 26.00

Vase
Marked: USA
$18.00 – 20.00

Vase
Marked: USA
$22.00 – 24.00

Vase
Marked: USA
$22.00 – 24.00

Vase
Marked: USA
$20.00 – 22.00

Jug
Marked: USA
$18.00 – 20.00

Jug
Marked: USA
$18.00 – 20.00

Jug
Marked: USA
$18.00 – 20.00

Jug
Marked: USA
$18.00 – 20.00

Jug
Marked: USA
$18.00 – 20.00

Jug
Marked: USA
$18.00 – 20.00

Jug
Marked: USA
$20.00 – 22.00

Pig
No Mark
$24.00 – 26.00

Bear
No Mark
$24.00 – 26.00

Cat
No Mark
$24.00 – 26.00

Dog
No Mark
$24.00 – 26.00

Puppy
No Mark
$24.00 – 26.00

Dachshund
No Mark
$24.00 – 26.00

Rabbit
No Mark
$24.00 – 26.00

Bunny
No Mark
$24.00 – 26.00

Bear
Marked: USA
$24.00 – 26.00

Lion
No Mark
$24.00 – 26.00

Snail
Marked: USA
$26.00 – 28.00

Frog
No Mark
$20.00 – 22.00

Turtle
No Mark
$24.00 – 26.00

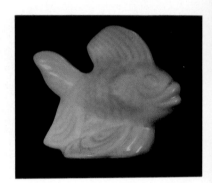

Fish
No Mark
$20.00 – 22.00

Tropical Fish
No Mark
$24.00 – 26.00

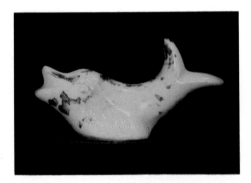

Fish
No Mark
$20.00 – 22.00

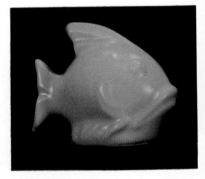

Fish
No Mark
$20.00 – 22.00

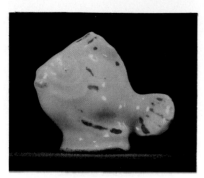

Fish
No Mark
$20.00 – 22.00

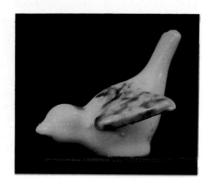

Flying Bird
No Mark
$20.00 – 22.00

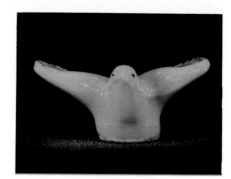

Bird
No Mark
$20.00 – 22.00

Sitting Bird
No Mark
$18.00 – 20.00

Parrot
No Mark
$18.00 – 20.00

Chicken
No Mark
$18.00 – 20.00

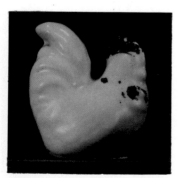

Rooster
No Mark
$20.00 – 22.00

Duck
No Mark
$22.00 – 24.00

Duck – Head Up
No Mark
$18.00 – 20.00

Duck – Head Down
No Mark
$18.00 – 20.00

Sitting Swan
No Mark
$18.00 – 20.00

Swan
No Mark
$18.00 – 20.00

Elephant
No Mark
$20.00 – 22.00

Pony
No Mark
$20.00 – 22.00

Horse
Marked: USA
$20.00 – 22.00

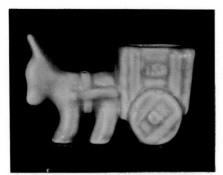

Donkey with Cart
Marked: USA
$20.00 – 22.00

Donkey with Basket
Marked: USA
$20.00 – 22.00

Donkey
No Mark
$20.00 – 22.00

Squirrel
No Mark
$70.00 – 75.00
Gold/$125.00 – 175.00

Raccoon
No Mark
$70.00 – 75.00
Gold/$125.00 – 175.00

Rabbit
No Mark
$70.00 – 75.00
Gold/$125.00 – 175.00

Tumbling Bear
No Mark
$70.00 – 75.00
Gold/$125.00 – 175.00

Puppy Dog
No Mark
$70.00 – 75.00
Gold/$125.00 – 175.00

Pekingese
No Mark
$70.00 – 75.00
Gold/$125.00 – 175.00

Deer
No Mark
$95.00 – 100.00
Gold/$150.00 – 225.00

BANKS

Howdy Doody 6¹/₂"
Marked: Bob Smith USA
$500.00 – 550.00

Howdy Doody 6¹/₂"
Marked: Bob Smith USA
$500.00 – 550.00

The Howdy Doody Bank was made in 1957. It was produced approximately one year, at which time production was stopped due to a trademark infringement.

Bull Dog 4¹/₂"
$200.00 – 225.00

Tumbling Bear 4¹/₂"
$200.00 – 225.00

CLOCKS

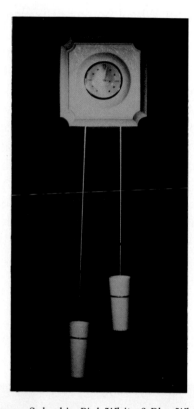

The Granddaughter clock is 10" square. It is semi-porcelain in two-tone ceramic with hand-etched decorations. The copper weight rods hold matching ceramic planters.

Pattern name – Suburbia, Pink/White & Blue/White – Shown above
Pattern name – Heritage, Brown/White – Not Shown
$175.00 – 200.00

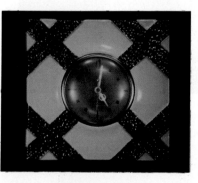

Medallion
Pink/Medallion or
Turquoise/Medallion
$90.00 – 110.00

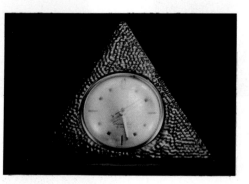

Pyramid
Medallion Finish
$150.00 – 175.00

Trellis
Green/White or
Brown/White
$90.00 – 110.00

BOOKENDS

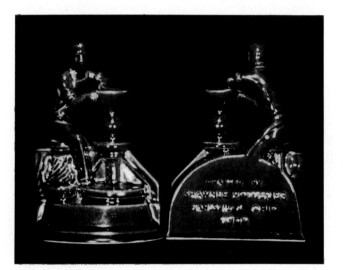

Potter Wheel
$550.00/Pair

The Potter Wheel bookends were designed in 1938 by Rudy Ganz. They were originally designed for and marked RumRill Pottery. The vases on the Potter Wheel bookends are duplicates of three RumRill vases that Shawnee had also designed for George RumRill. In 1960, long after Shawnee had ceased making pottery for the RumRill Pottery Company, the bookends were once again manufactured. The marking was changed to: Crafted by Shawnee Potteries/Zanesville, Ohio 1960. They were not offered for sale but were given out at pottery shows and to important visiting guests. Later, the bookends were produced by Terrace Ceramics with the markings changed accordingly.

Flying Geese/Gold
Marked: Shawnee 4000
$50.00 – 75.00

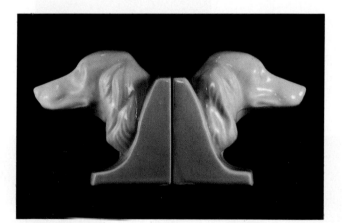

Dog Heads
Marked: USA
$50.00 – 75.00

CIGARETTE BOXES

Arrowhead
Marked: Shawnee
Rare

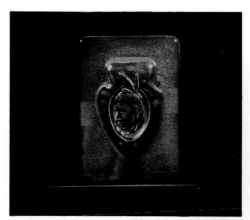

Arrowhead
Marked: Shawnee
$500.00 – 600.00

The Arrowhead Cigarette Box is also available in White with a Burgundy arrowhead and a Blue Indian head. The ashtray was given as a promotional item at pottery shows and to buyers and visitors.

Solid Color
Marked: USA 682
Surf and Ebony with Gold Trim
$35.00 – 45.00

Confetti
Marked: Kenwood USA 2120
Pink/Black, White/Black, Turquoise/Black
$35.00 – 45.00

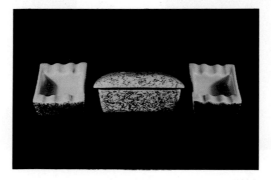

Kashäni
Cigarette Box, Marked: Kenwood USA 3016
Ashtray, Marked: Kenwood USA 3018
Black/Gold, White/Gold, Red/Gold
$55.00 – 60.00 set

ASHTRAYS

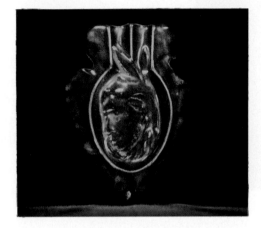

The Arrowhead ashtray was designed in 1937. Embossed with the company logo, the ashtray and matching cigarette box were given out as promotional items at pottery shows and to visiting buyers and salesmen.

Arrowhead
Marked: Shawnee
$225.00 – 250.00

The Hostess Ashtray Line came in 21 different colors and treatments on seven different designs. The retailer could purchase the Hostess Line in a Master Assortment, which consisted of 156 pieces, or an Introductory assortment which consisted of 78 pieces.

The Contemporary Ashtray Line had unique modern shapes and came in pink and turquoise. They were designed to make cigarettes fall into the tray. As with most of the Shawnee ashtrays, they came with flocked (felted) bottoms to protect the furniture.

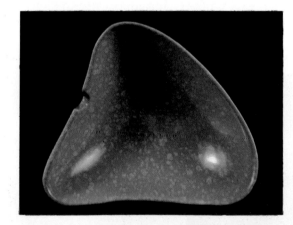

Trio 5" Hostess Line
Marked: Shawnee USA 201
Aqua, Sand, Lime
$12.00 – 14.00

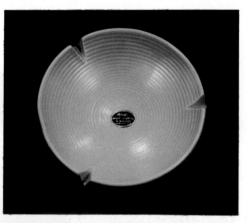

Ribbed 5"
Marked: Shawnee USA 202
Green, Pink
$10.00 – 12.00

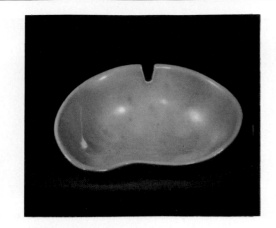

Oblong 5"
Marked: Shawnee USA 203
Aqua, Pink
$6.00 – 8.00

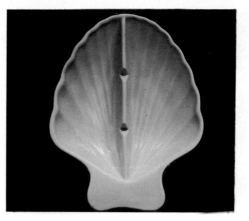

Shell
Marked: Shawnee USA 204
Green, Pink, White
$20.00 – 25.00

Flight 8½" Hostess Line
Marked: Shawnee USA 205
Pink/Gold, Black/Gold, Turquoise/Gold
$10.00 – 12.00

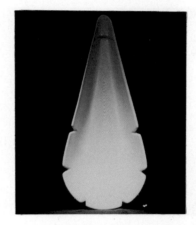

Decorator 11¾"
Marked: Shawnee USA 206
Green, Pink, White
$20.00 – 25.00

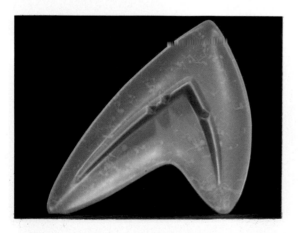

Flight 11" Hostess Line
Marked: Shawnee USA 208
Blonde, Mist Green, Carnation
$14.00 – 16.00

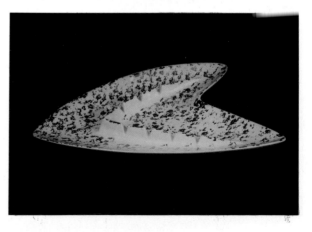

Flight 13"
Marked: Shawnee USA 209
Pink/Gold, Black/Gold, Turquoise/Gold
$16.00 – 18.00

Oval 5" Hostess Line
Marked: Shawnee USA 210
Onyx, Bronze, Greenfire
$16.00 – 18.00

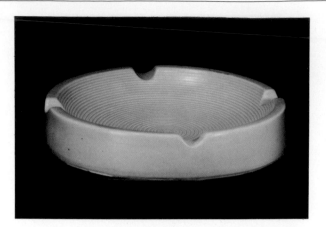

Ribbed 8½"
Marked: Shawnee USA 214
Green, Pink
$16.00 – 18.00

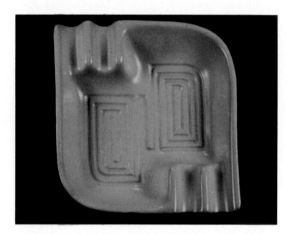

Double 5" Hostess Line
Marked: Shawnee USA 216
White, Pink, Turquoise
$4.00 – 6.00

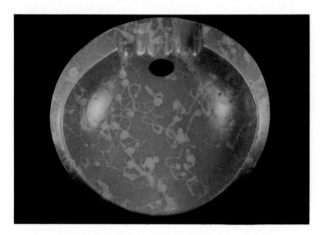

Studio 6½" Hostess Line
Marked: Shawnee USA 219
Blonde, Ice Blue, Carnation, Earthtones
$8.00 – 10.00

Geometric 5" Artique Line
Marked: Shawnee USA 251
White/Gold, Black/Gold
$18.00 – 20.00

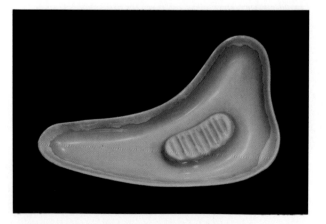

Boomerang 11" Contemporary Line
Marked: Shawnee USA 300
Bermuda Turquoise, Carnation Pink
$10.00 – 12.00

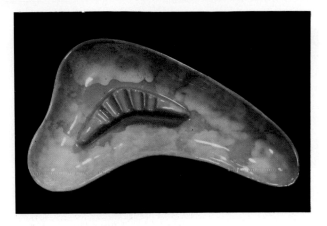

Modern 11" Hostess Line
Marked: Shawnee USA 301
Aqua, Pink, Yellow with Cloud Treatment
$12.00 – 15.00

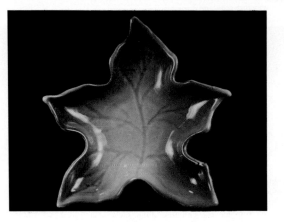

Leaf
Marked: USA 350
Multi-Color
$6.00 – 8.00

Rectangular Double
Marked: USA 401
White, Turquoise, Pink with vining
$8.00 – 10.00

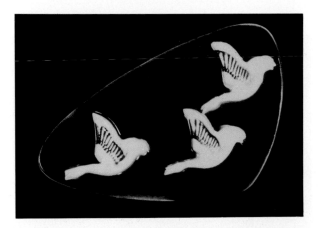

Flying Geese
Marked: USA 403
Black and White
$16.00 – 18.00

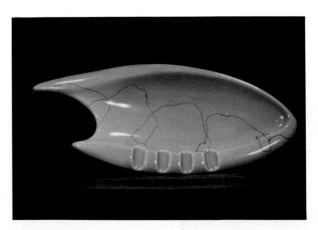

Modern 10½" Contemporary Line
Marked: USA 407
Vined Turquoise or Pink
$18.00 – 20.00

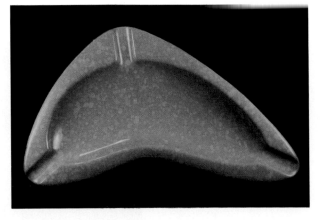

Flair 9¼ Contemporary Line
Marked: USA 408
Stardust, Turquoise or Pink
$12.00 – 15.00

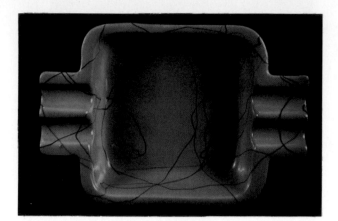

Square 5¼" Contemporary Line
Marked: Shawnee USA 409
Vined Turquoise or Pink
$6.00 – 8.00

Rectangular 5"
Marked: Shawnee USA 410
Stardust, Turquoise or Pink
$4.00 – 6.00

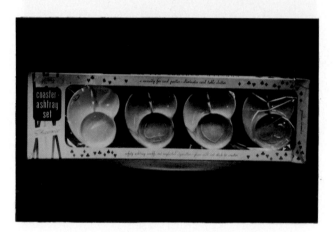

Coaster/Ashtray in Box
Marked: USA 411
Heart, Spade, Club, Diamond Turquoise, Pink, Green, Yellow
$90.00 – 100.00 in box; $15.00 – 18.00 each

Coaster/Ashtray
Marked: Pat. Pending Shawnee USA
Heart, Spade, Club, Diamond/Red or Black
$22.00 – 24.00 each

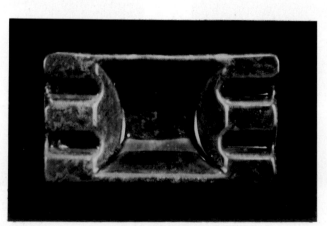

Rectangular 5"
Marked: USA 681
$6.00 – 8.00

Panther
Marked: Kenwood USA 2201
Black and White
$25.00 – 27.00

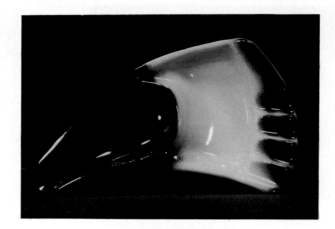

Panther Paw
Marked: USA
Black and White
$25.00 – 27.00

Geometric 5" Artique Line
Marked: Shawnee USA
White/Gold, Black/Gold
$12.00 – 14.00

Magnolia Blossom
Marked: USA
White, Flax Blue, Old Ivory, Dusty Rose
$18.00 – 20.00

Squirrel
Marked: USA
Blue, Turquoise, Yellow, White
$26.00 – 28.00

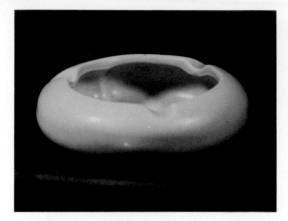

Round
Marked: USA
$6.00 – 10.00

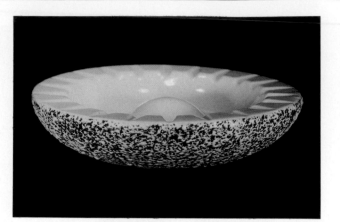

Monte Carlo 11"
Marked: Kenwood USA 2125
Pink and Charcoal, White and Black
$20.00 – 25.00

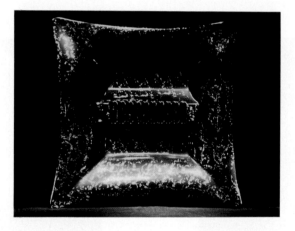

Rivera 17"
Marked: Kenwood USA 3101
Black and Gold, White and Gold
$20.00 – 25.00

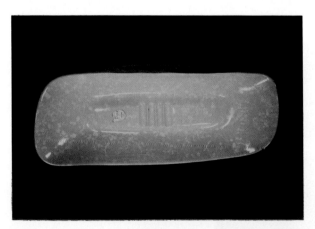

Oblong 16 x 6
Marked: USA
Pink and Turquoise with a Tiara Treatment
$26.00 – 28.00

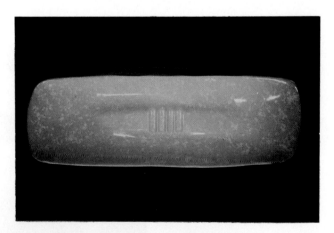

Rectangular 17 x 6
Marked: USA 3519
Pink and Turquoise with a Tiara Treatment
$26.00 – 28.00

LAMPS

Researching the lamps has not been an easy task. Although Shawnee made many lamps, most of them were made for other companies. Therefore, they cannot be found in Shawnee literature and articles. The only way to positively identify them would be to know which companies hired Shawnee to make lamps, and then research those particular companies. We have been able to identify the lamps shown partly from literature, but mostly from former employees. We have found several common denominators: they are all glazed inside, they all have glazed bottoms, and they all have an inner ring on the bottom, often referred to as an inner strength ring. Several lamps very similar to the Shawnee lamps have been found, however, that do not have all three of the above mentioned traits. Don't be fooled by these! We have shown the bottoms of several of the lamps, in hopes that this will help in identifying.

Deer
No Mark
$45.00 – 50.00

Puppy
No Mark
$75.00 – 100.00

Bow Tie
No Mark
$45.00 – 50.00

Ballerina
No Mark, $65.00 – 70.00
The Ballerina should be sitting on a base.

Double Victorian
No Mark
$50.00 – 55.00

Victorian Lady
No Mark
$35.00 – 40.00

Victorian Man
No Mark
$35.00 – 40.00

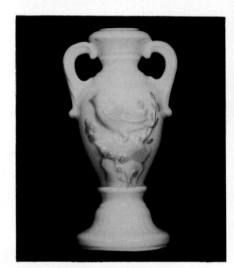

Bluebirds Embossed
No Mark
$45.00 – 50.00

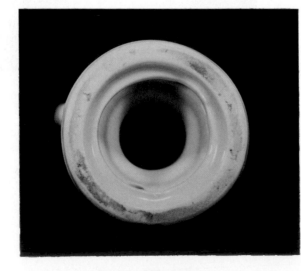

Bottom of Bluebird Lamp

Flowers Embossed
No Mark
$45.00 – 50.00

Embossed Oriental
No Mark
$45.00 – 50.00

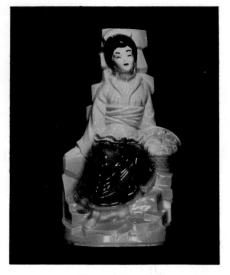

Harvest Queen
No Mark
$55.00 – 60.00

Harvest King
No Mark
$50.00 – 55.00

Girl with Mandolin – Low Base
No Mark
$30.00 – 35.00

Boy with Mandolin
No Mark
$30.00 – 35.00

Girl with Mandolin – High Base
No Mark
$30.00 – 35.00

Flamingo Dancers
No Mark
$40.00 – 45.00

Double Orientals
No Mark
$40.00 – 45.00

Bottom of Double Orientals

Moors – Male and Female/Gold
No Mark
$110.00 – 120.00 for pair

Natives – Male and Female
No Mark
$80.00 – 100.00 for pair

Duck – Cold Paint
No Mark
$60.00 – 65.00

Elephant – Cold Paint
No Mark
$60.00 – 65.00

Clown – Cold Paint
No Mark
$60.00 – 65.00

Embossed Wall Lamp
No Mark
$130.00 – 135.00

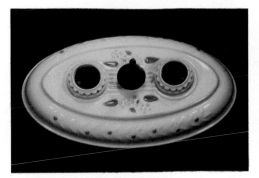

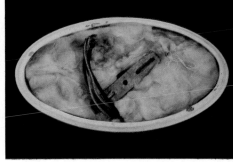

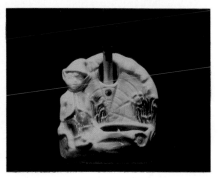

Embossed Ceiling Lamp
No Mark
$60.00 – 65.00

Back of Ceiling Lamp

Elf Planter Wall Lamp
No Mark, Has Glazed Back
$55.00 – 60.00

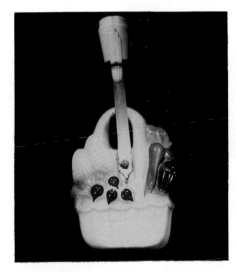

Vegetable Wall Lamp
No Mark, Has Glazed Back
$55.00 – 60.00

Fruit Wall Lamp
No Mark, Has Glazed Back
$55.00 – 60.00

Mother Goose
No Mark

We have pictured the Mother Goose lamp because it has been collected as Shawnee. However, we have not been able to verify that it is actually Shawnee. There are six variations of this lamp.

ARTIQUE CERAMIC PLAQUES

Artique Plaques were available in two styles and 12 colors: Green, Tan, Cinnamon, Yellow, Lemon Yellow, Pink, Melba, Blue, Turquoise, Gray, Black, and White. They were designed to have a three dimensional effect. When laid together, they could construct numerous design patterns.

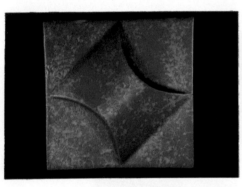

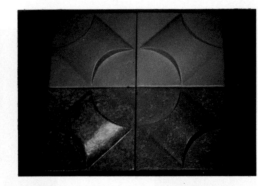

There is no photo available for the second style. It is rectangular in shape, measuring 11¾"x7¾", with a raised football shape design in the center.

Artique Ceramic Plaque
7¾" x 7¾"
$15.00 – 18.00

Four plaques laid together to form a design

VISTA-FLEX CERAMIC PLAQUES

Vista-Flex also was available in two styles and in the same 12 colors as the Artique Plaques.

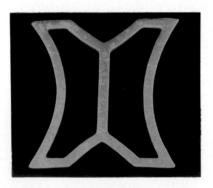

There is no photo available for the second style. It is square in shape, measuring 3¾" x 3¾".

Vista-Flex
7¾" x 7¾"
$15.00 – 18.00

RONDO BATHROOM ACCESSORIES

Rondo colors available: Gray, Green, Blue, Yellow, Pink, Melba, Tan, Cinnamon, Lemon Yellow, Black, and White.

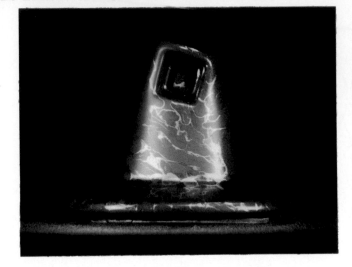

Towel Holder
Test Piece in avocado with gold vining

Bottom of Towel Holder Test Piece
with color formula written in gold

Soap Dish with Grab Bar	$12.00 – 15.00	Tumbler and Toothbrush Holder	$12.00 – 15.00
Paper Holder with Plastic Roller	$12.00 – 15.00	Towel Bar Set	
Soap Dish	$12.00 – 15.00	(one bar with two holders)	$12.00 – 15.00

SIMPLEX BATHROOM ACCESSORIES

Simplex consisted of five bathroom accessories in Gray, Green, Blue, Yellow, Pink, Melba, Tan, Cinnamon, Lemon Yellow, Black, or White. Unlike the other bathroom accessories that Shawnee made, these pieces have a flush back. They were glued on the wall, rather than being recessed into the wall. All pieces are marked USA.

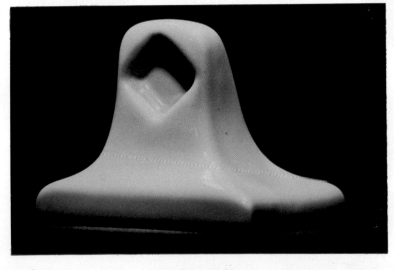

Towel Bar Holder
$12.00 – 15.00 for a set

Other pieces available:
Soap Dish with Grab Bar $12.00 – 15.00
Soap Dish $12.00 – 15.00
Tumbler and Toothbrush Holder $12.00 – 15.00

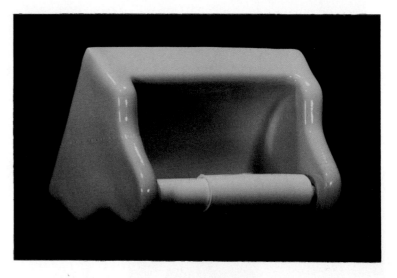

Paper Holder
$12.00 – 15.00

There is another bathroom accessory line by Shawnee. However, we have not been able to determine the name of the line. Its shape is similar to the Simplex, except it has a raised back that would be recessed in the wall. It is also marked with a USA along with a 200, 201, 202, 203, or 204 number. These numbers indicated the stock number of the piece.

Other pieces available:
Soap Dish with Grab Bar $12.00 – 15.00
Paper Holder $12.00 – 15.00
Tumbler and Toothbrush Holder $12.00 – 15.00
Towel Bar Set $12.00 – 15.00

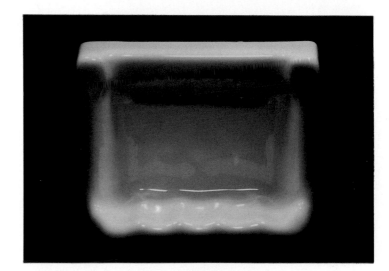

Soap Dish
Marked: USA 200
$12.00 – 15.00

MISCELLANEOUS

Tracts

Back of Tracts

Incense Burner/Gold
Marked: USA
$60.00 – 65.00
No Gold $90.00 – 100.00

These booklets (tracts) were located in a tract rack in the lobby of the Shawnee factory. The tracts covered a variety of topics and were free for the taking. Several hundred tracts have been found, all dating from the late 1940's to the late 1950's. All of the tracts are rubber stamped with "Shawnee Pottery, Zanesville, Ohio."

Darning Egg with
Darn Aid Label
No Mark
Pink or Blue
$85.00 – 90.00

Fish, Plant Waterer
Marked: USA
$35.00 – 40.00

Bird, Plant Waterer
Marked: USA
$35.00 – 40.00

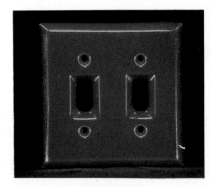

Light Switch Plate
No Mark
We feel sure that this was available in
other colors, however, a box of them
was located, and all were in brown.
$35.00 – 40.00

CAMEO

Introduced in 1960, Cameo is a line of planters and vases made of high fired ceramics in satin matt glazes with a delicately textured surface. The colors we have listed were the original colors available. However, Ebony and Lavender were added at a later date.

Flower Blowl Planter 5"
Marked: Shawnee USA 2501
Citrus Green, Jonquil Yellow, Shell Pink, Ebony
$10.00 – 12.00

Flower Bowl Planter 6"
Marked: Shawnee USA 2502
Platinum Gray, Butterscotch, Wedgwood Blue
$10.00 – 12.00

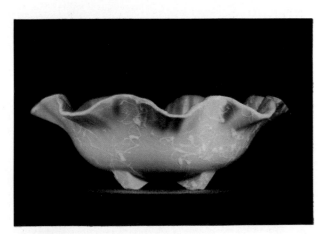

Centerpiece Planter 10"
Marked: Shawnee USA 2503
Citrus Green, Butterscotch, Mint Green
$12.00 – 15.00

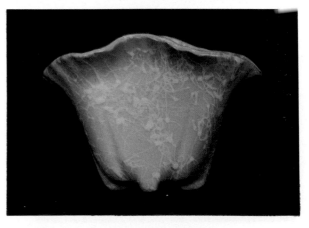

Fan Planter 6½"
Marked: Shawnee USA 2504
Jonquil Yellow, Satin Green
$12.00 – 14.00

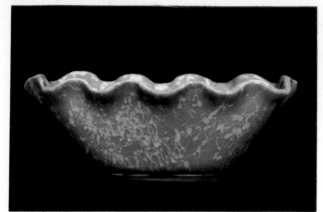

Windowbox 10"
Marked: Shawnee USA 2505
Citrus Green, Shell Pink, Wedgwood Blue
$10.00 – 12.00

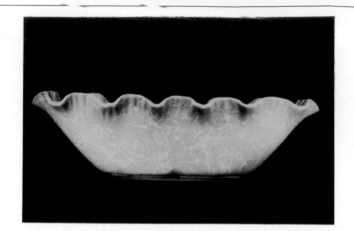

Windowbox 14"
Marked: Shawnee USA 2506
Platinum Gray, Butterscotch, Mint Green
$12.00 – 14.00

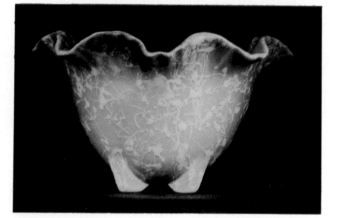

Urn Planter 8½"
Marked: Shawnee USA 2507
Citrus Green, Shell Pink, Mint Green
$12.00 – 14.00

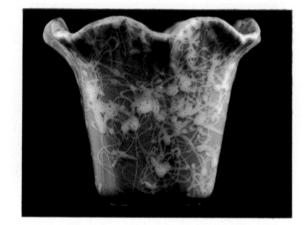

Jardiniere 4"
Marked: Shawnee USA 2508
Citrus Green, Wedgwood Blue, Satin White
$8.00 – 10.00

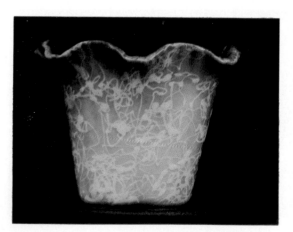

Jardiniere 5"
Marked: Shawnee USA 2509
Jonquil Yellow, Butterscotch, Mint Green
$10.00 – 12.00

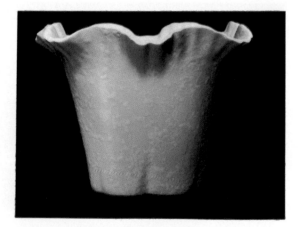

Jardiniere 7"
Marked: Shawnee USA 2511
Platinum Gray, Butterscotch, Mint Green
$16.00 – 18.00

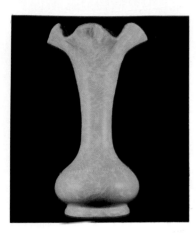

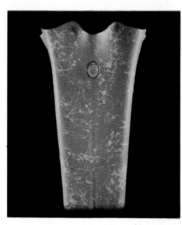

Flower Vase 9"
Marked: Shawnee USA 2512
Platinum Gray, Mint Green,
Jonquil Yellow
$12.00 – 14.00

Bouquet Vase 11"
Marked: Shawnee USA 2515
Platinum Gray, Butterscotch,
Mint Green
$10.00 – 12.00

Flower Vase 12"
Marked: Shawnee USA 2516
Citrus Green, Shell Pink,
Satin White
$12.00 – 14.00

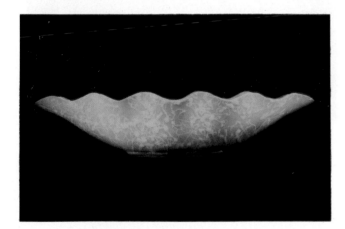

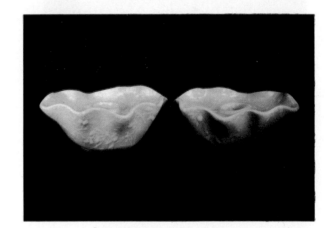

Console Bowl 15"
Marked: Shawnee USA 2517
Satin Green, Blonde, Satin White
$12.00 – 14.00

Candle holders
Marked: Shawnee USA 2518
Satin Green, Blonde, Satin White
$15.00 – 20.00

Other pieces available:

Jardiniere, 6"	Shawnee USA 2510	Citrus Green, Shell Pink, Satin Green	$12.00 – 14.00
Bouquet Vase, 9"	Shawnee USA 2513	Citrus Green, Shell Pink, Wedgwood Blue	$10.00 – 12.00
Flared Vase, 10"	Shawnee USA 2514	Shell Pink, Satin Green, Satin White	$14.00 – 16.00
Ashtray, 12"	Shawnee USA	Satin White, Blonde, Satin Green	$18.00 – 20.00

All the jardinieres were made to fit companion size red clay pots.

CHANTILLY

Chantilly was introduced in 1958. It was described as a cascade of ceramic lace over capacious designs. The bases were painted brass color to give the piece an expensive look.

Scalloped Planter 3½"
Marked: Shawnee USA 1801
Red, Lime, Holland Blue
$10.00 – 12.00

Oblong Planter 7½"
Marked: Shawnee USA 1803
Lemon, Dove Gray, Snow White
$10.00 – 12.00

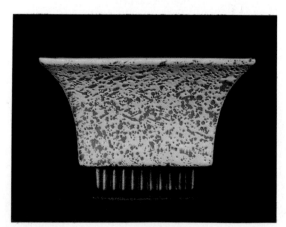

Square Planter 5"
Marked: Shawnee USA 1804
Turquoise, Glen Green, Forest Green, Cinnamon
$10.00 – 12.00

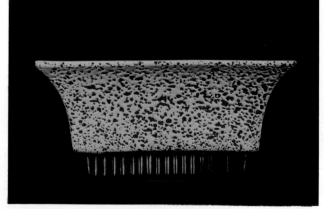

Square Planter 7"
Marked: Shawnee USA 1806
Snow White, Cinnamon, Forest Green
$10.00 – 12.00

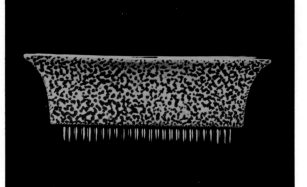

Flared Jardiniere 4½"
Marked: Shawnee USA 1807
Red, Holland Blue, Dove Gray
$10.00 – 12.00

Rectangular Windowbox 9"
Marked: Shawnee USA 1810
Red, Holland Blue, Dove Gray
$10.00 – 12.00

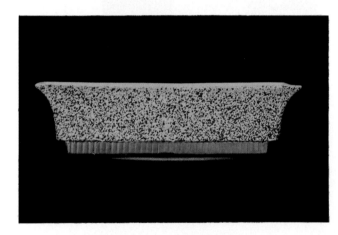

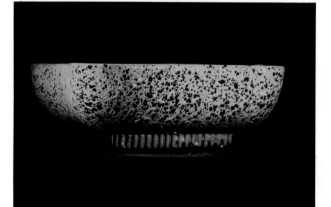

Rectangular Windowbox 12"
Marked: Shawnee USA 1811
Turquoise, Wintergreen, Confetti Pink
$10.00 – 1200

Centerpiece Planter 10"
Marked: Shawnee USA 1813
Holland Blue, Dove Gray, Glen Green
$10.00 – 12.00

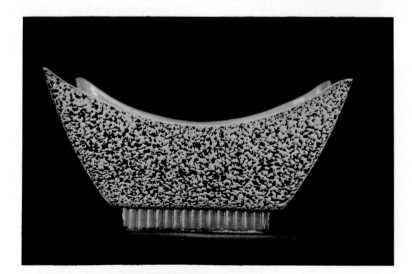

Pagoda Planter 12"
Marked: Shawnee USA 1814
Turquoise, Wintergreen, Confetti Pink
$12.00 – 14.00

Floral Vase 8"
Marked: Shawnee USA 1817
Wintergreen, Turquoise, Confetti Pink
$10.00 – 12.00

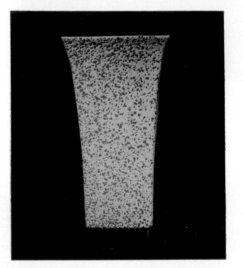

Bouquet Vase 9"
Marked: Shawnee USA 1818
Cinnamon, Snow White, Forest Green
$10.00 – 12.00

Other pieces available:

Pulpit Planter, 4½"	Shawnee USA 1802	Tangerine, Wintergreen Confetti Pink	$8.00 – 10.00
Square Planter, 6"	Shawnee USA 1805	Confetti Pink, Dove Gray, Wintergreen	$7.00 – 9.00
Flared Jardiniere, 6½"	Shawnee USA 1808	Wintergreen, Confetti Pink, Turquoise	$10.00 – 12.00
Flared Jardiniere, 8"	Shawnee USA 1809	Snow White, Cinnamon, Forest Green	$10.00 – 12.00
Rectangular Windowbox, 12"	Shawnee USA 1811	Turquoise, Wintergreen, Confetti Pink	$10.00 – 12.00
Rectangular Windowbox, 15"	Shawnee USA 1812	Snow White, Cinnamon, Forest Green	$12.00 – 14.00
Console Planter, 17½"	Shawnee USA 1815	Snow White, Cinnamon, Forest Green	$14.00 – 16.00
Bud Vase, 10"	Shawnee USA 1816	Lime, Carnation, Lemon	$10.00 – 12.00
Bouquet Vase, 11"	Shawnee USA 1820	Cinnamon, Snow White, Forest Green	$10.00 – 12.00

The jardinieres were made to fit companion size red clay pots.

CHERIE ARTWARE

Cherie is not to be confused with Petit-Point. Six pieces were taken from the Petit-Point line, and they have the same 1900 number series as the Petit-Point. The difference is the color. Cherie Artware was created for late fall and Christmas merchandising; therefore, it was made available in the bright autumn colors of Golden Oak, Bittersweet, Maple Blaze, Hickory Brown, Holly Red, and Autumn Green, offset by a white glazed interior and a gold decorated base.

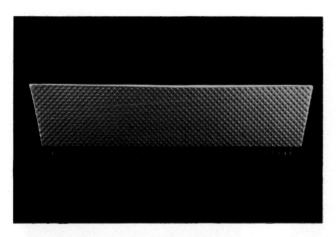

Windowbox 11"
Marked: Shawnee USA 1906
Hickory Brown
$8.00 – 10.00

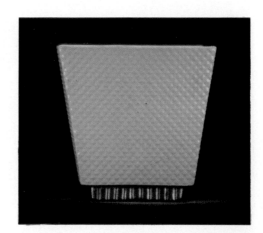

Jardiniere 5"
Marked: Shawnee USA 1908
Autumn Green
$8.00 – 10.00

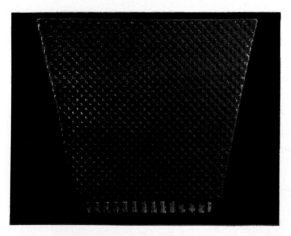

Jardiniere 6"
Marked: Shawnee USA 1909
Holly Red
$10.00 – 12.00

Other pieces available:

Square Planter, 5"	Shawnee USA 1902	$8.00 – 10.00
Square Planter, 7"	Shawnee USA 1904	$10.00 – 12.00
Windowbox, 8"	Shawnee USA 1905	$10.00 – 12.00

CONFETTI

Confetti has a nubby texture on the outer surface to give it a 3-D effect. It was originally available with Pink glaze on Charcoal, and White glaze on Black. Later Chartreuse glaze on Brown was added to the line.

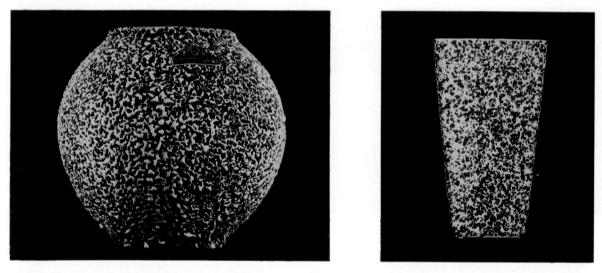

Globe Vase
Marked: Kenwood USA 2100
$10.00 – 12.00

Vase 8"
Marked: Kenwood USA 2102
$10.00 – 12.00

Vase 10"
Marked: Kenwood USA 2103
$12.00 – 14.00

Jardiniere 5"
Marked: Kenwood USA 2106
$10.00 – 12.00

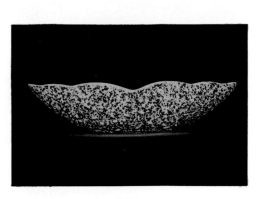

Oval Bowl 11"
Marked: Kenwood USA 2110
$10.00 – 12.00

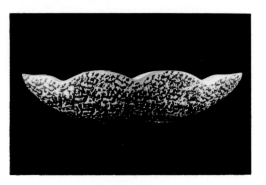

Oval Bowl 14¹/₂"
Marked: Kenwood USA 2112
$12.00 – 14.00

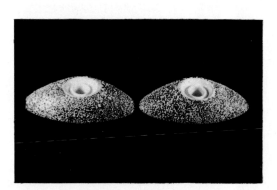

Candle Holders 6³/₄"
Marked: Kenwood USA 2113
$20.00 – 25.00

Planting Dish 7¹/₂"
Marked: Kenwood USA 2114
$8.00 – 10.00

Flower Bowl 10¹/₂"
Marked: Kenwood USA 2117
$12.00 – 14.00

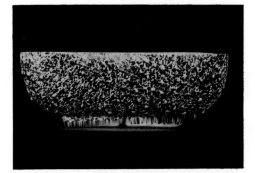

Flower Bowl 8"
Marked: Kenwood USA 2116
$10.00 – 12.00

Cigarette Box and Ashtrays
Marked: Kenwood USA 2120 and 2122
Box $30.00 – 35.00; Ashtrays $18.00 – 20.00 each

Other pieces available:
Jardiniere, 4" Kenwood USA 2105 $10.00 – 12.00
Monte Carlo Ashtray – Shown in the Ashtray Section

145

ELEGANCE

Urn Planter 5"
Marked: Shawnee USA 1401
Golden Beige, Satin Pink, Coral
$12.00 – 14.00

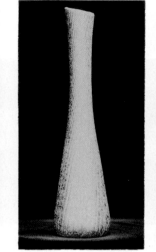

Bud Vase 11"
Marked: Shawnee USA
1402
Golden Beige Crystal,
Green, Satin Pink
$10.00 – 12.00

Square Windowbox 4"
Marked: Shawnee USA 1404
Turquoise, Bittersweet, Tropical Green
$10.00 – 12.00

Freeform Planter 7"
Marked: Shawnee USA 1406
Bittersweet, Tropical Green, Canary
$10.00 – 12.00

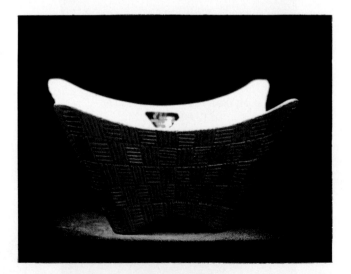

Flared Planter 8½"
Marked: Shawnee USA 1407
Golden Beige, Bittersweet, Coral
$12.00 – 14.00

Modern Vase 9"
Marked: Shawnee USA 1408
Sterling White, Sable, Crystal Green
$12.00 – 14.00

Classic Flower Bowl 6"
Marked: Shawnee USA 1409
Sterling White, Golden Beige, Satin Pink
$10.00 – 12.00

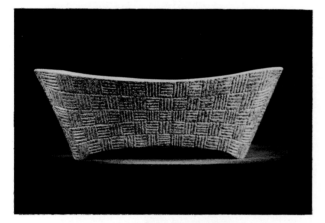

Windowbox 9"
Marked: Shawnee USA 1410
Sable, Crystal Green, Satin Pink
$12.00 – 14.00

Cone Planter 7" With Brass Plated Stand
No Mark
Golden Biege, Bittersweet, Turquoise
$50.00 – 55.00

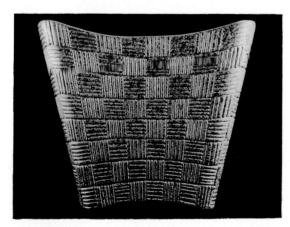

Jardiniere 6"
Marked: Shawnee USA 1412
Sterling White, Sable, Crystal Green
$10.00 – 12.00

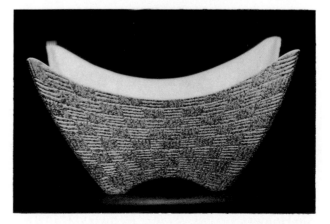

Flared Planter 12"
Marked: Shawnee USA 1413
Sterling White, Golden Beige, Bittersweet
$12.00 – 14.00

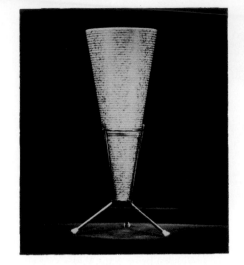

Cone Vase 12"
With Brass Plated Stand
No Mark
Sable, Golden Beige, Crystal Green
$55.00 – 60.00

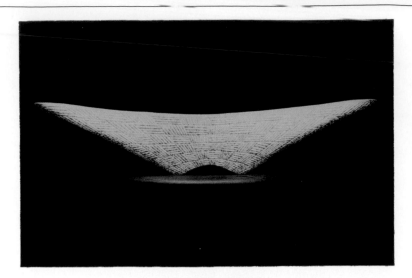

Console Planter 18"
Marked: Shawnee USA 1417
Sterling White, Golden Beige, Crystal Green
$12.00 – 14.00

Shell Flower Bowl 8"
Marked: Shawnee USA 1418
Sterling White, Turquoise, Satin Pink
$12.00 – 14.00

Other pieces available:

Jardiniere, 5"	Shawnee USA 1403	Sterling White, Sable, Crystal Green	$10.00 – 12.00
Pedestal Planter, 5"	Shawnee USA 1405	Golden Beige, Satin Pink, Coral	$14.00 – 16.00
Window Box, 14"	Shawnee USA 1415	Sable, Turquoise, Satin Pink	$12.00 – 14.00
Jardiniere, 7"	Shawnee USA 1416	Sterling White, Sable, Crystal Green	$14.00 – 16.00
Candle Holders	Kenwood USA 1419		$22.00 – 24.00

FAIRY WOOD

Fairy Wood was introduced in 1957. It has a wood texture exterior, which was achieved by actually making the molds out of plywood.

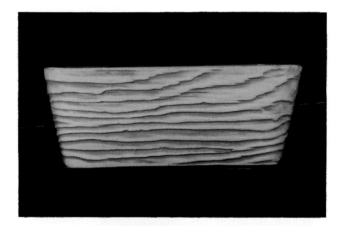

Square Planter 7"
Marked: Shawnee USA 1204
Blossom Pink, Turquoise, Jonquil Yellow
$8.00 – 10.00

Rectangular Windowbox 9"
Marked: Shawnee USA 1205
White, Blonde, Orchid
$8.00 – 10.00

Rectangular Windowbox 12"
Marked: Shawnee USA 1206
Blossom Pink, Turquoise, Jonquil
$10.00 – 12.00

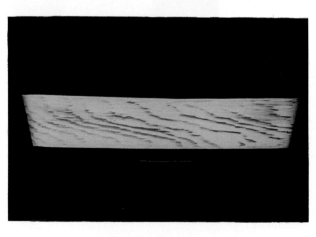

Rectangular Windowbox 15"
Marked: Shawnee USA 1207
Meadow Green, Apricot, Driftwood Gray
$10.00 – 12.00

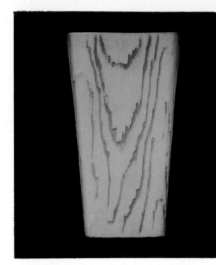

Vase 8"
Marked: Shawnee USA 1208
Turquoise, Blossom Pink, Blonde
$8.00 – 10.00

Vase 9"
Marked: Shawnee USA 1209
Apricot, Apple Green, Driftwood Gray
$10.00 – 12.00

Modern Vase 10"
Marked: Shawnee USA 1210
Turquoise, Blossom Pink, Blonde
$10.00 – 12.00

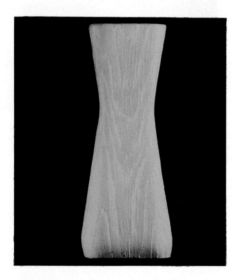

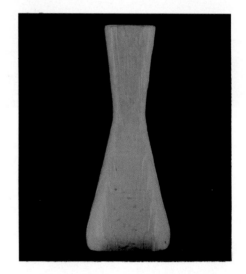

Modern Vase 11"
Marked: Shawnee USA 1211
Apricot, Apple Green, Driftwood Gray
$12.00 – 14.00

Modern Vase 8½"
Marked: Shawnee USA 1212
Blossom Pink, Blonde, Apple Green
$10.00 – 12.00

Other pieces available:

Square Planter, 4½"	Shawnee USA 1201	White, Blonde, Orchid	$6.00 – 8.00
Square Planter, 5"	Shawnee USA 1202	Blossom Pink, Turquoise, Jonquil Yellow	$6.00 – 8.00
Square Planter, 6"	Shawnee USA 1203	Meadow Green, Apricot, Driftwood Gray	$8.00 – 10.00

FERNWARE

The Fernware is available in Pink, Turquoise, Beige, Green, White, Yellow, and Ebony.

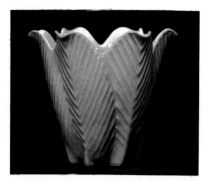

Planter 5"
Marked: USA 1701
$8.00 – 10.00

Flower Bowls 7½"
Marked: USA 1702
$8.00 – 10.00 each

Square Planter 7"
Marked: USA 1703
$10.00 – 12.00

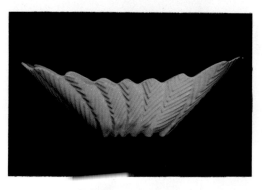

Windowbox 11½"
Marked: USA 1705
$12.00 – 14.00

Other pieces available:

Windowbox, 8"	USA 1704	$8.00 – 10.00
Windowbox, 14"	USA 1706	$10.00 – 12.00
Jardiniere, 4"	USA 1707	$8.00 – 10.00
Jardiniere, 5"	USA 1708	$10.00 – 12.00
Jardiniere, 6"	USA 1709	$12.00 – 14.00

KASHÄNI

Kashäni is a semi-porcelain ceramic. The glazes are high fired with a decorated bisque finish. It was available in three colors: Persian Red with gold, Black with gold and White with gold. The interiors are glazed in complementary colors. The stands are triple plated brass.

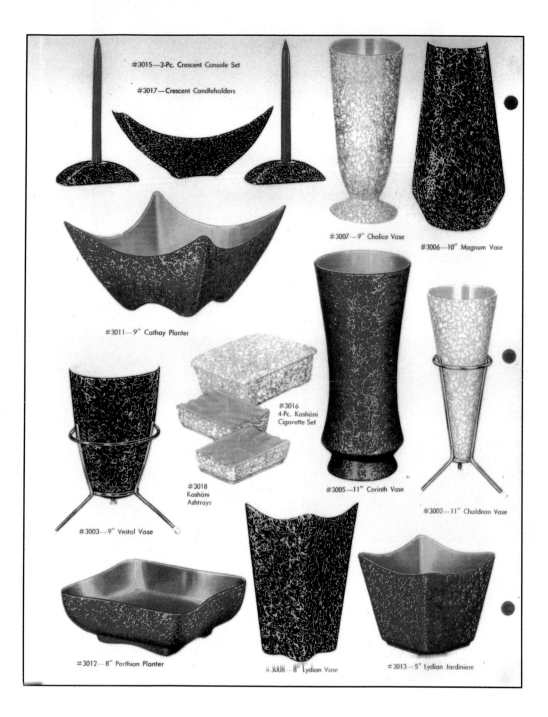

#3015—3-Pc. Crescent Console Set

#3017—Crescent Candleholders

#3007—9" Chalice Vase

#3006—10" Magnum Vase

#3011—9" Cathay Planter

#3016 4-Pc. Kashäni Cigarette Set

#3018 Kashäni Ashtrays

#3005—11" Corinth Vase

#3002—11" Chaldean Vase

#3003—9" Vestal Vase

#3012—8" Parthian Planter

#3008—8" Lydian Vase

#3013—5" Lydian Jardiniere

Other pieces available:

3001	Chaldean Vase, 14"	$30.00 – 35.00	3008	Lydian Vase, 8"	$22.00 – 24.00
3002	Chaldean Vase, 11"	$30.00 – 35.00	3012	Parthian Planter, 8"	$20.00 – 22.00
3003	Vestal Vase, 9"	$30.00 – 35.00	3013	Lydian Jardiniere, 5"	$20.00 – 22.00
3004	Persian Planter, 7"	$30.00 – 35.00	3014	Lydian Jardiniere, 4"	$20.00 – 22.00
3005	Corinth Vase, 11"	$26.00 – 28.00	3016	Cigarette Box	$30.00 – 35.00
3006	Magnum Vase, 10"	$26.00 – 28.00	3017	Candle Holders (pair)	$26.00 – 28.00
3007	Chalie Vase, 9"	$26.00 – 28.00	3018	Ashtray	$8.00 – 10.00

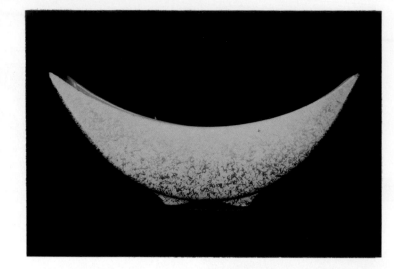

Crescent Planter 14"
Marked: Kenwood USA 3009
$16.00 – 18.00

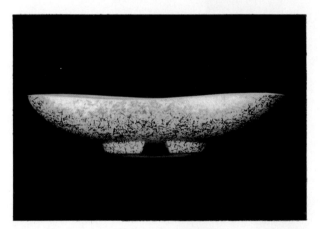

Elysian Planter 14"
Marked: Kenwood USA 3010
$12.00 – 14.00

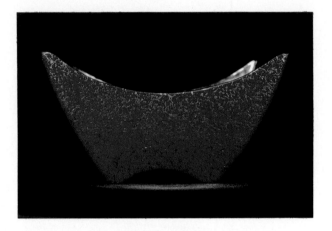

Cathay Planter 9"
Marked: Kenwood USA 3011
$18.00 – 20.00

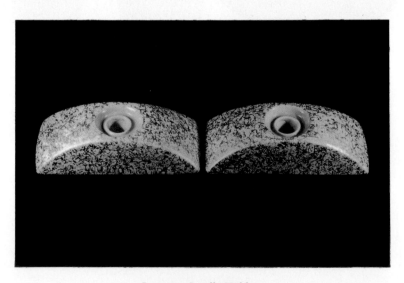

Crescent Candle Holders
Marked: Kenwood USA 3017
$20.00 – 22.00

LIANA

Introduced in 1957, Liana is most easily recognized by its Copper, Silver, or Gold vining.

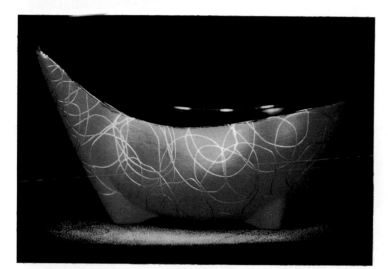

Freeform Planter 7"
Marked: Shawnee USA 1007
Chinese Red, Lemon Yellow, Turquoise
Copper interior
$12.00 – 14.00

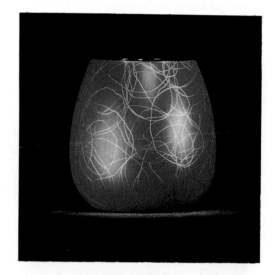

Pineapple Planter 4½"
Marked: Shawnee USA 1008
Chinese Red, Lemon Yellow, Turquoise
Copper interior
$12.00 – 14.00

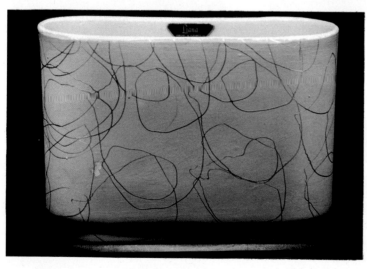

Pillow Vase 7x5"
Marked: Shawnee USA 1012
Lime with Yellow interior, Flamingo with White interior,
Turquoise with Pink interior
$10.00 – 12.00

Bud Vase 8½"
Marked: Shawnee USA 1014
Lime with Yellow interior,
Flamingo with White interior,
Turquoise with Pink interior
$10.00 – 12.00

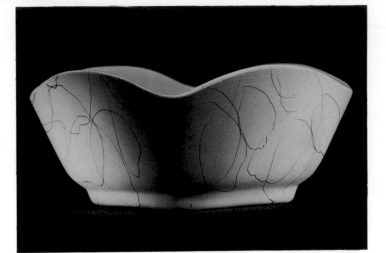

Symmetric Planter 8½"
Marked: Shawnee USA 1018
Lime with Yellow interior, Flamingo with White interior,
Turquoise with Pink interior
$12.00 – 14.00

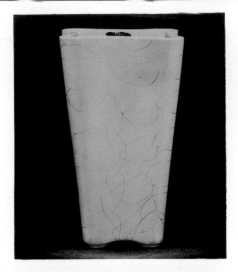

Modern Vase 9¼"
Marked: Shawnee USA 1021
Pink with White interior, White with Pink
interior, Black with White interior
$10.00 – 12.00

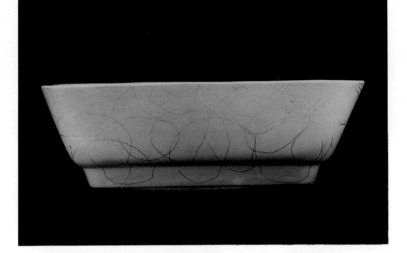

Casement Planter 9¼"
Marked: Shawnee USA 1019
Lime with Yellow interior,
Flamingo with White interior, Turquoise with Pink interior
$12.00 – 14.00

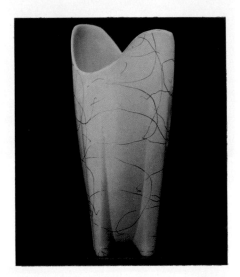

Decorator Vase 9¼"
Marked: Shawnee USA 1023
Pink with White interior, White with Pink
interior, Black with White interior
$10.00 – 12.00

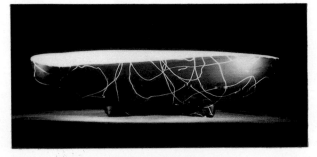

Gourd Planter 11½"
Marked: Shawnee USA 1025
Pink with White interior, White with Pink interior
Black with White interior
$12.00 – 14.00

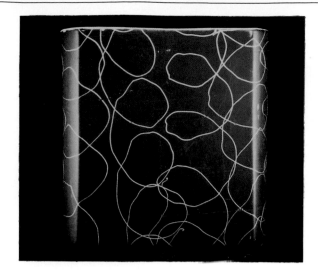

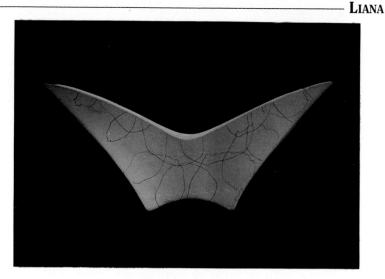

Tall Pillow Vase 6¼" x 7¼"
Marked: Shawnee USA 1026
Pink with White interior, White with Pink interior
Black with White interior
$12.00 – 14.00

Flight Planter 13"
Marked: Shawnee USA 1027
Pink with White interior, White with Pink interior
Black with White interior
$12.00 – 14.00

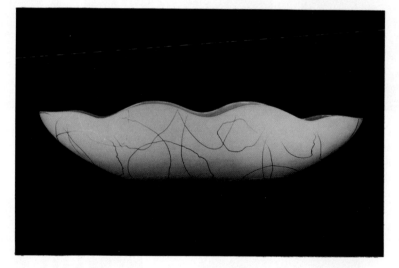

Console Planter 13"
Marked: Shawnee USA 1028
Pink with White interior, White with Pink interior
Black with White interior
$12.00 – 14.00

Other pieces available:

Teabox, 4"

| | Shawnee USA 1003 | Chinese Red, Turquoise, Lemon Yellow with copper interiors | $12.00 – 14.00 |

Saddle Planter, 5"

| | Shawnee USA 1004 | Chinese Red, Turquoise, Lemon Yellow with copper interiors | $12.00 – 14.00 |

Scalloped Planter, 7½"

| | Shawnee USA 1005 | Chinese Red, Turquoise, Lemon Yellow with copper interiors | $12.00 – 14.00 |

Crosscut Planter, 5"

| | Shawnee USA 1006 | Chinese Red, Turquoise, Lemon Yellow with copper interiors | $12.00 – 14.00 |

Cucumber Planter, 11½"

| | Shawnee USA 1011 | Lime with Yellow, Flamingo with White, Turquoise with Pink | $10.00 – 12.00 |

Floral Vase, 8"

| | Shawnee USA 1017 | Lime with Yellow, Flamingo with White, Turquoise with Pink | $10.00 – 12.00 |

MEDALLION

The Medallion Line was introduced in 1957. It is a bronze glaze that makes the pieces appear to be cast bronze. The items on which the bronze glaze was used were pre-existing designs. Pieces with an asterisk were designs from 1954 and 1955.

Flower Pot Liner
Experimental piece
Marked: Shawnee USA 465, 6029 ABCD
$25.00 – 30.00

*Rooster Planter 6"
Marked: Shawnee USA 503
$85.00 – 95.00

*Prairie Planter 10½"
Marked: Kenwood USA 1511 &
Shawnee USA
$100.00 – 110.00

Tankard
Marked: USA 990
$50.00 – 60.00

Vase 8"
Marked: Kenwood USA 1513
$40.00 – 45.00

Other pieces available:

Urn Planter, 5"	#1501	$40.00 – 45.00	*Pony Planter, 8½"	#1509	$75.00 – 80.00
Leaf Planter, 5"	#1502	$40.00 – 45.00	Flower Bowl, 14½"	#1510	$45.00 – 50.00
Egyptian Planter, 11½"	#1504	$45.00 – 50.00	Flair Planter, 14½"	#1512	$40.00 – 45.00
*Butterfly Planter, 8½"	#1505	$45.00 – 50.00			
*Basketweave Planter, 9½"	#1506	$45.00 – 50.00			
*Shell Planter, 8"	#1507	$40.00 – 45.00			
Window Box Planter, 15"	#1508	$45.00 – 50.00			

There are more Medallion vases than shown, however, we were unable to verify all of them.

PASTEL MEDALLION

This Medallion line is available in satin pastels of peppermint Pink, Green and White.

Hammered Vase 9"
Marked: Kenwood USA 1514
$22.00 – 24.00

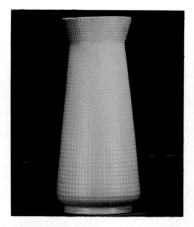

Decorator Vase 11"
Marked: Kenwood USA 1516
$22.00 – 24.00

Gladiola Vase 12"
Marked: Kenwood USA 1517
$22.00 – 24.00

Flower Bowl 14½"
Marked: Kenwood USA 1510
$22.00 – 24.00

Other pieces available:

Urn Planter, 5"	1501	$20.00 – 22.00	Shell Planter, 8"	1507	$20.00 – 22.00
Leaf Planter, 5"	1502	$20.00 – 22.00	Windowbox Planter, 15"	1508	$20.00 – 22.00
Egyptian Planter, 11½"	1504	$20.00 – 22.00	Flair Planter, 14½"	1512	$20.00 – 22.00
Butterfly, 8½"	1505	$18.00 – 20.00	Bouquet Vase, 8"	1513	$22.00 – 24.00
Basketweave Planter, 9½"	1506	$18.00 – 20.00	Provincial Vase, 10"	1515	$22.00 – 24.00

PETIT-POINT

Petit-Point was made in geometric designs with an embossed pattern. The exterior is simulated brass with black decorated bases. All have white glazed interiors.

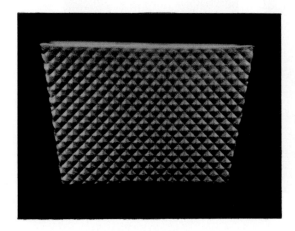

Square Planter 4"
Marked: USA 1901
$6.00 – 8.00

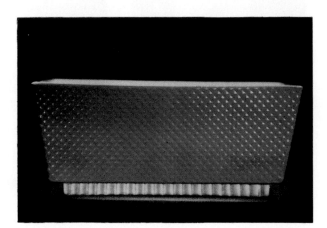
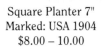

Square Planter 7"
Marked: USA 1904
$8.00 – 10.00

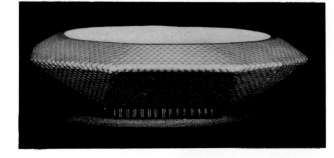

Octagon Flower Bowl 10"
Marked: USA 1911
$10.00 – 12.00

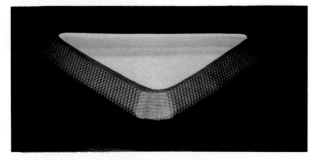

Triangle Flower Bowl 11"
Marked: USA 1912
$10.00 – 12.00

Other pieces available:

Square Planter, 5"	USA 1902	$8.00 – 10.00	Windowbox, 14"	USA 1907	$12.00 – 14.00
Square Planter, 6"	USA 1903	$10.00 – 12.00	Jardiniere, 5"	USA 1908	$10.00 – 12.00
Window Box, 8"	USA 1905	$10.00 – 12.00	Jardiniere, 6"	USA 1909	$12.00 – 14.00
Window Box, 11"	USA 1906	$12.00 – 14.00	Jardiniere, 7"	USA 1910	$14.00 – 16.00

STARDUST

The Stardust Line consisted of a new glaze applied to eight previously designed pieces. Colors: Pink, Chartreuse, Avocado, and Surf.

Other pieces available:

Oval Bowl	Shawnee USA 2001	$18.00 – 20.00	Shell Planting Dish	Shawnee USA 2005	$18.00 – 20.00
Oval Bowl	Shawnee USA 2002	$20.00 – 22.00	Planting Dish	Shawnee USA 2007	$18.00 – 20.00
Planting Dish	Shawnee USA 2004	$18.00 – 20.00	Vase, 8"	Shawnee USA 2012	$22.00 – 24.00
			Vase, 10"	Shawnee USA 2014	$22.00 – 24.00

Vase 10"
Marked: Shawnee USA 2013
$24.00 – 26.00

Stardust
by KENWOOD

the stuff dreams are made of

describes these semi-porcelain creations that turn bouquets into floral masterpieces. A color to complement any blossom or plant . . . a style for any occasion. All bases flocked (felted) to protect fine furniture.

Furnished in the following colors:
   Pink • Chartreuse • Avocado • Surf

Specify colors when ordering

NUMBER		CARTON PACK	CARTON WEIGHT	RETAIL EACH
2001	Oval Bowl 2¾"x11"x3"	12 pcs.	13 lbs.	$1.25
2002	Oval Bowl 3½"x14½"x5¼" . .	6 pcs.	13 lbs.	2.00
2004	Planting Dish 3"x7⅞"x7⅞" . .	12 pcs.	25 lbs.	1.75
2005	Shell			
	Planting Dish 4¼"x8"x5¾"	12 pcs.	25 lbs.	1.50
2007	Planting Dish 2¾"x7½"x3½"	18 pcs.	19 lbs.	1.00
2012	Vase 8" high	12 pcs.	25 lbs.	1.50
2013	Vase 10" high	12 pcs.	50 lbs.	2.50
2014	Vase 10" high	12 pcs.	52 lbs.	2.50

KENWOOD CERAMICS
Division of Shawnee Potteries, Zanesville, Ohio, U.S.A.

TIARA

Tiara is available in colors of Bamboo Green, Lilac, Blonde, Jonquil Yellow, Pumpkin, Forest Green, Cornflower, Blue, Violet, Bermuda Green, Sandalwood, Lime, Velvet Pink, Turquoise, and Pearl White, all muted with white accents.

African Violet Planter 6½"
Marked: Shawnee USA 3503
$15.00 – 18.00

African Violet Planter 7½"
Marked: Shawnee USA 3504
$15.00 – 18.00

Crown Jardiniere 8"
Marked: Shawnee USA 3505
$15.00 – 18.00

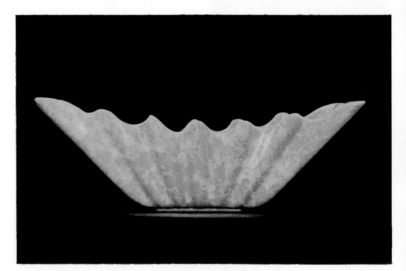

Flared Windowbox 11½"
Marked: Shawnee USA 3507
$14.00 – 16.00

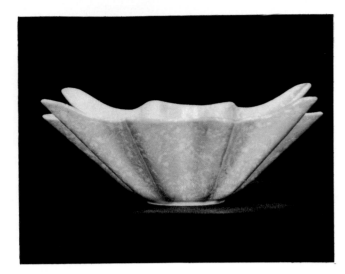

Arbor Flower Bowl 10½"
Marked: Shawnee USA 3509
$14.00 – 16.00

Crown Vase 8"
Marked: Shawnee USA 3511
$12.00 – 14.00

Arbor Vase 9"
Marked: Shawnee USA 3512
$12.00 – 14.00

Modern Vase 10"
Marked: Shawnee USA 3510
$14.00 – 16.00

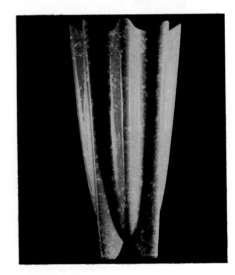

Arbor Vase 11"
Marked: Shawnee USA 3514
$14.00 – 16.00

Other pieces available:

Arbor Planter, 6"	Shawnee USA 3501	$14.00 – 16.00
Crown Planter, 6"	Shawnee USA 3502	$10.00 – 12.00
Crown Jardiniere, 8"	Shawnee USA 3506	$14.00 – 16.00
Flared Window Box, 14½"	Shawnee USA 3508	$14.00 – 16.00
Bud Vase, 11"	Shawnee USA 3510	$12.00 – 14.00
Crown Vase, 12"	Shawnee USA 3515	$14.00 – 16.00

TOUCHÉ

Touché was introduced in 1956. Pieces 1001 – 1006 were available in Aztec Red, Custard, and Turquoise with Copper interiors. Pieces 1011 – 1016 came in Lime with Yellow interiors, Tweed with Ivory interiors, and Wildflower with Pink interiors. Pieces 1021 – 1026 came in Salt and Pepper with White interiors, Seafoam with White interiors, and Teaberry with Pink interiors. There are 18 pieces in this design line.

Teabox Planter 4"
Marked: Shawnee USA 1003
$4.00 – 6.00

Crosscut Planter 4¾"
Marked: Shawnee USA 1006
$6.00 – 8.00

Cucumber Planter 11½"
Marked: Shawnee USA 1011
$8.00 – 10.00

Pillow Vase 7"
Marked: Shawnee USA 1012
$8.00 – 10.00

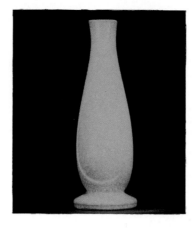

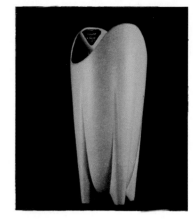

Bouquet Vase 8¼"
Marked: Shawnee USA 1013
$10.00 – 12.00

Bud Vase 8½"
Marked: Shawnee USA 1014
$10.00 – 12.00

Decorator Vase 9¼"
Marked: Shawnee USA 1023
$12.00 – 14.00

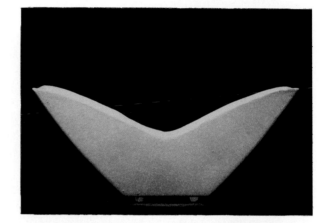

Flair Planter 9"
Marked: Shawnee USA 1022
$10.00 – 12.00

Gondola Windowbox 12"
Marked: Shawnee USA 1024
$12.00 – 14.00

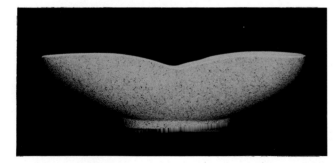

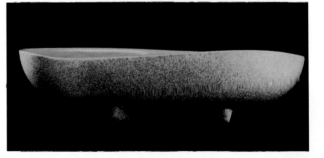

Wing Planter 11"
Marked: Shawnee USA 1015
$8.00 – 10.00

Gourd Planter 11½"
Marked: Shawnee USA 1025
$12.00 – 14.00

Other pieces available:

Pillow Planter, 4"	Shawnee USA 1001	$6.00 – 8.00
Double Planter, 6¾"	Shawnee USA 1002	$8.00 – 10.00
Saddle Planter, 5"	Shawnee USA 1004	$8.00 – 10.00
Scalloped Planter, 7½"	Shawnec USA 1005	$8.00 – 10.00
Cucumber Planter, 11½"	Shawnee USA 1011	$8.00 – 10.00
Conventional Planter, 9½"	Shawnee USA 1016	$10.00 – 12.00

FERN KITCHENWARE

This kitchenware has an octagonal shape, embossed with conventional fern leaf design on panels. The colors available are Yellow, Flax Blue, and Turquoise, except the mixing bowls, which came in two additional colors of Dusty Rose and Old Ivory. All the pieces are marked with a USA.

Cookie Jar and Cover
4 quart
$75.00 – 85.00

Canister and Cover
2½" quart
$65.00 – 70.00

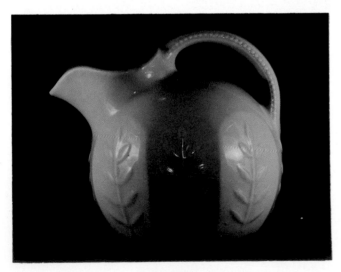

Ball Jug
2 quart
$45.00 – 50.00

Tea Pot
2 cups
$75.00 – 85.00

Tea Pot
6 cups
$75.00 – 85.00

Creamer
9 ounce
$35.00 – 45.00

Coffee Maker, 5 cups
French Drip type with coffee basket, water holder,
and water spreader, lid fits both pot and water holder
$90.00 – 95.00

Sugar
9 ounce
$35.00 – 45.00

Salt and Pepper
7 ounce
$40.00 – 45.00

Pitcher
1½ pint
$60.00 – 70.00

Mixing Bowls 5", 6", 7", 8", 9"
6" and 8" not shown
$75.00 – 85.00 for set

Match Box Holder
$110.00 – 120.00

Salt Box and Cover
$125.00 – 130.00

Grease Jar and Cover
16 ounces
$55.00 – 60.00

SNOWFLAKE KITCHENWARE

This kitchenware has a snowflake design. The smaller pieces were given out as premiums by Proctor and Gamble. All of the pieces, except the mixing bowls and batter bowls, came in colors of Old Ivory, Turquoise, Flax Blue, and Yellow. Old Ivory was dropped soon after the start of production. The mixing bowls and batter bowls came in Burgundy, Dark Green, Old Ivory, Dark Blue, and Yellow.

In October 1942 the entire Snowflake line except the bowls was dropped from production. At that time, the colors of the bowls were changed to Yellow, Flax Blue, Dusty Rose, Old Ivory, and Turquoise Green. Except for the salt and pepper, all pieces are marked with a USA.

Canister
2 quart
$45.00 – 55.00

Ball Jug
2 quart
$35.00 – 45.00

Mixing Bowls
Consisted of a 5", 6", 7", 8", and 9"
$75.00 – 85.00 set

Batter Bowl
$20.00 – 25.00

Utility Pitcher
24 ounce, 5¹/₈" high
$40.00 – 45.00

Salt and Pepper
4", has 6 and 7 holes or holes that form an S and P
$20.00 – 25.00

Grease Jar
3¹/₂"
$40.00 – 45.00

Creamer and Sugar
7 ounce
$25.00 – 35.00 set

Tea Pot
2 Cup
$50.00 – 55.00

Tea Pot
5 Cup
$55.00 – 60.00

Tea Pot
8 Cup
$60.00 – 65.00

FLOWER AND FERN KITCHENWARE

This kitchenware has an embossed flower and fern leaf design. It comes in Yellow, Flax Blue, Turquoise, Old Ivory, Dark Green, Dark Blue, and Burgundy. The pieces are marked with a USA.

Pitcher
4 Cup
$22.00 – 24.00

Tea Pot
2 Cup
$35.00 – 40.00

Tea Pot
6 Cup
$40.00 – 45.00

Coffee Maker, 5 Cup
French Drip Style with coffee basket and water holder
$75.00 – 85.00

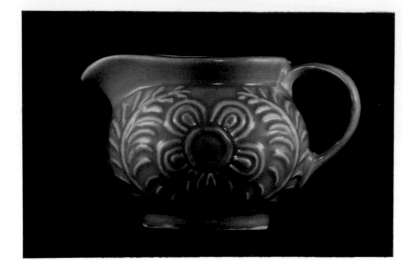

Creamer
$20.00 – 25.00

Sugar
$20.00 – 25.00

Creamer
$18.00 – 20.00

Aladdin Style Creamer
$20.00 – 22.00

Aladdin Style Sugar
$20.00 – 22.00

Salt and Pepper 5"
$15.00 – 18.00 Not Shown, 4" $22.00 – 24.00

Grease Jar
$40.00 – 45.00

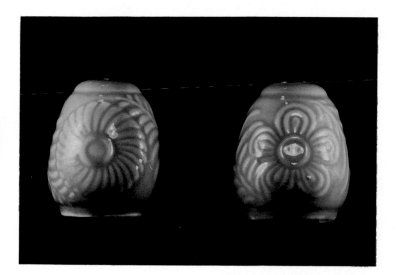

Salt and Pepper 3"
$22.00 – 24.00

Salt Box
$85.00 – 90.00

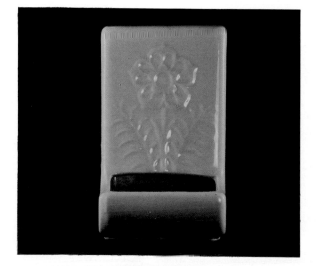

Match Box Holder
$95.00 – 105.00

Pot and Liner 3"
$10.00 – 12.00

Pot and Liner 4¼"
$10.00 – 12.00

Jardiniere 2¼"
$6.00 – 8.00

Jardiniere 4"
$12.00 – 15.00

Jardiniere 7"
$25.00 – 30.00

VALENCIA

Several months after Shawnee opened, Sears Roebuck and Company sent their housewares stylist, Jane Miller, a division merchandise manager, F.R. Henniger, and their pottery buyer, James Butler, to Zanesville to help design a kitchenware and dinnerware line for them. Working closely with Shawnee designer Louise Bauer, they created the Valencia Line. Sears gave a 20-piece starter set with each new refrigerator sold. The starter set and other Valencia pieces could also be ordered from the Sears Roebuck catalog.

Valencia was in production from 1937 to 1940. It was originally produced in Blue, Green, Yellow, and Tangerine. A year after the start of production, the Burgundy was added. The prices ranged from 12 cents for the A.D. saucer to $1.98 for the five-piece waffle set. The Tangerine pieces were from 2 to 50 cents more per piece.

Occasionally, you will find a piece marked Valencia or USA, however the majority of the pieces are unmarked.

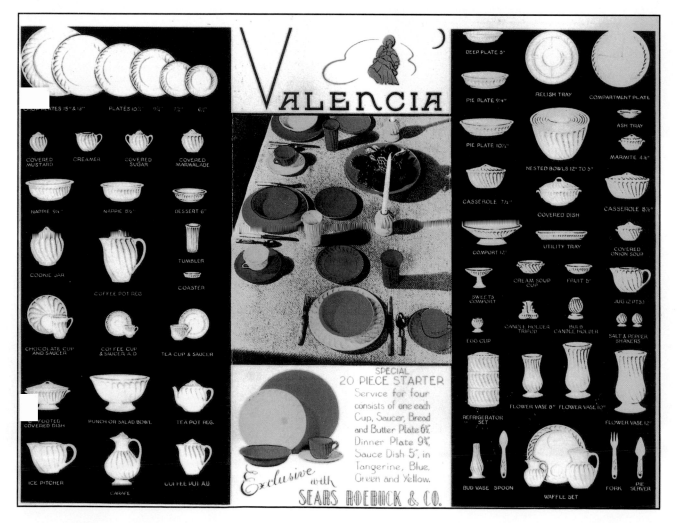

175

Nappie 8¹/₂"
No Mark
$15.00 – 20.00

Nappie 9¹/₂"
No Mark
$15.00 – 20.00

Fruit Bowl 5"
No Mark
$15.00 – 20.00

Three of the eight Nesting Bowls
No Mark
$18.00 – 20.00 each

Ice Pitcher
Marked: USA
$35.00 – 40.00

Tea Pot, Regular
No Mark
$55.00 – 65.00

Carafe, No Lid
No Mark
$40.00 – 45.00

Coffee Pot, Regular No Lid
No Mark
$35.00 – 40.00

Cup and Saucer A.D.
No Mark
$20.00 – 22.00 set

Tea Cup and Saucer
No Mark
$16.00 – 18.00 set

Plates 6½"
No Mark
$10.00 – 12.00

Chop Plate 13", Plate 10¾"
No Mark
Chop Plate $20.00 – 25.00, 10¾" Plate $12.00 – 14.00

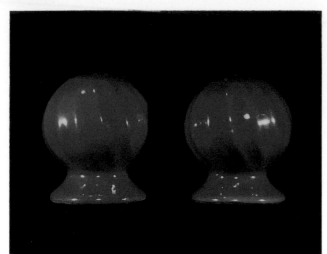

Salt and Pepper
No Mark
$25.00 – 30.00 set

Creamer
Marked: Valencia
$12.00 – 14.00

Covered Sugar Bowl
No Mark
$20.00 – 25.00

Egg Cup
No Mark
$14.00 – 16.00 each

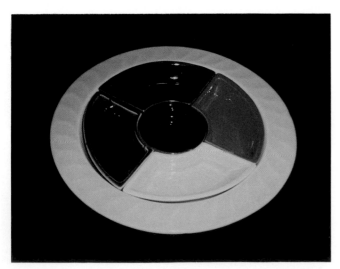

Relish Tray 10½"
No Mark
$130.00 – 135.00

Bulb Type Candle Holder
No Mark
$18.00 – 20.00 for single

Coasters
No Mark
$12.00 – 15.00

Bud Vase
No Mark
$15.00 – 17.00

Other pieces available:

Ashtray	$12.00 – 14.00	Fruit Bowl	$15.00 – 20.00
Bowls, Nesting, 5" – 12"	$18.00 – 20.00	Ice Pitcher	$30.00 – 35.00
Bud Vase	$12.00 – 14.00	Jug 2 pts.	$25.00 – 30.00
Candle Holders, Bulb, pair	$30.00 – 35.00	Marmite, 4½"	$22.00 – 24.00
Candle Holders, Tripod, pair	$35.00 – 40.00	Covered Mustard	$25.00 – 30.00
Carafe w/lid	$45.00 – 50.00	Nappie, 8½"	$15.00 – 20.00
Casserole, 7½"	$45.00 – 50.00	Nappie, 9½"	$15.00 – 20.00
Casserole, 8½"	$45.00 – 50.00	Onion Soup, Covered	$25.00 – 30.00
Chocolate Cup & Saucer	$25.00 – 27.00	Pie Plate, 10½"	$18.00 – 20.00
Chop Plate, 15"	$26.00 – 27.00	Pie Plate, 9¼"	$18.00 – 20.00
Chop Plate, 13"	$26.00 – 27.00	Pie Server	$50.00 – 55.00
Coaster, each	$12.00 – 15.00	Plate, 6½"	$10.00 – 12.00
Coffee Cup & Saucer A.D., set	$20.00 – 22.00	Plate, 7¾"	$10.00 – 12.00
Coffee Pot A.D.	$30.00 – 35.00	Plate, 9¾"	$12.00 – 14.00
Coffee Pot, Regular w/lid	$35.00 – 40.00	Plate, 10¾"	$12.00 – 14.00
Comport, 12"	$24.00 – 26.00	Plate, Compartment	$22.00 – 24.00
Comport, Sweets	$16.00 – 18.00	Plate, Deep, 8"	$12.00 – 14.00
Cookie Jar	$85.00 – 90.00	Punch Bowl, 12"	$28.00 – 30.00
Covered Dish	$25.00 – 30.00	Refrigerator Set	$65.00 – 75.00
Covered Dish, 8"	$30.00 – 35.00	Relish Tray	$130.00 – 135.00
Cream Soup Cup	$12.00 – 14.00	Salt and Pepper, set	$25.00 – 30.00
Creamer	$12.00 – 14.00	Spoon	$35.00 – 40.00
Dessert, 6"	$8.00 – 10.00	Covered Sugar	$20.00 – 22.00
Egg Cup	$14.00 – 16.00	Tea Cup & Saucer, set	$16.00 – 18.00
Flower Vase, 8"	$12.00 – 14.00	Tea Pot, Regular	$55.00 – 65.00
Flower Vase, 10"	$14.00 – 16.00	Utility Tray	$15.00 – 18.00
Fork	$30.00 – 35.00	Waffle Set, 5 pieces	$95.00 – 100.00

LOBSTER WARE

Lobster Ware was introduced in 1954. It was originally available in a Satin Charcoal or Glossy Van Dyke Brown. The color was later changed to a Glossy Black glaze. The line was not a huge success and was discontinued in 1956.

The Lobster Pins were a promotional item. They were given out at pottery shows and to visiting guests. Approximately 2½" long, they are stamped on the back with "Kenwood Ceramics, Shawnee Pottery, Zanesville, Ohio."

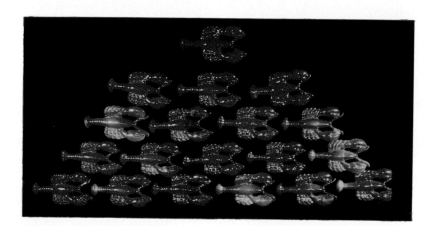

The 19 Lobster Pins
Courtesy of Juan and Bonita Klinehoffer
$65.00 – 75.00 each

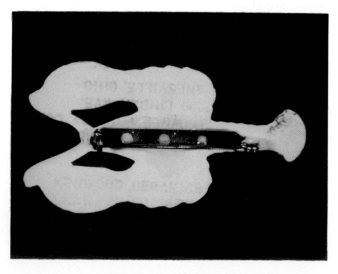

Back of Lobster Pin

Mugs 8 oz.
Marked: Kenwood USA 911
$75.00 – 85.00 each

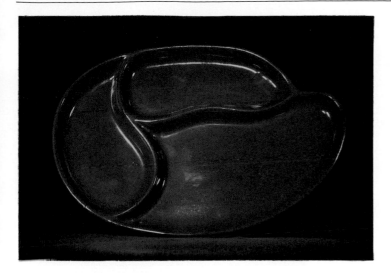

Compartment Plate; Marked: Kenwood USA 912
Pastel: Pink & Black, Yellow & Black, Green & Black, Ivory & Black
$75.00 – 100.00

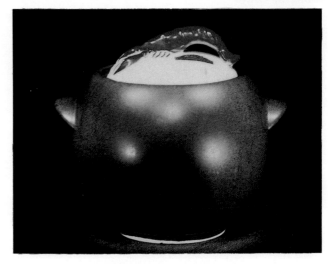
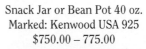

Snack Jar or Bean Pot 40 oz.
Marked: Kenwood USA 925
$750.00 – 775.00

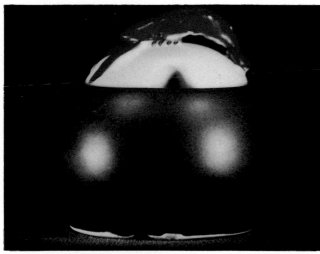

Covered Relish 5½"
Marked: Kenwood USA 926
$45.00 – 50.00

Butter Dish
Marked: Kenwood USA 927
$95.00 – 110.00

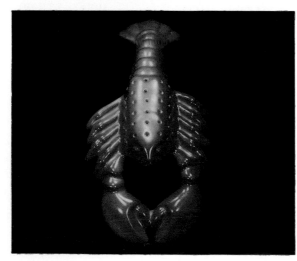

Hors d'oeuvre Holder 7¼"
Marked: USA
$250.00 – 275.00

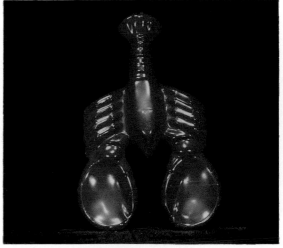

Double Spoon Holder 8½"
Marked: USA 935
$225.00 – 250.00

White French Casserole 2 qt.
Marked: 904; Rare color, we are aware of six sets made
$75.00 – 85.00

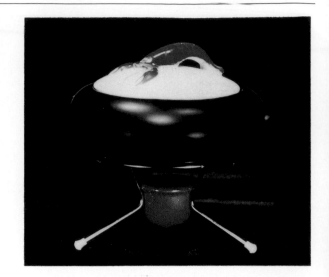

French Casserole in Triple Plated brass stand and
warmer, available in 10 oz, 16 oz, and 2 qt.
$65.00 – 70.00

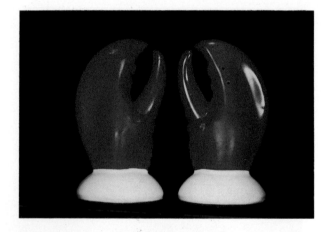

Claw Salt and Pepper
Marked: USA
$35.00 – 40.00

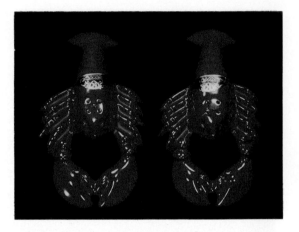

Full Body Salt and Pepper
Marked: USA
$200.00 – 225.00

Jug Type Salt and Pepper
Marked: USA
$100.00 – 110.00

Other pieces available:

French Casserole, 10 oz.	900	$18.00 – 21.00
8 pc. French Casserole Set in Box	901	$65.00 – 70.00
French Casserole, 16 oz.	902	$22.00 – 25.00
French Casserole, 2 qt.	904	$25.00 – 30.00
4 pc. Range Set in Box	906	$65.00 – 70.00
Covered Sugar or Utility Jar	907	$24.00 – 26.00
3 pc. Sugar and Creamer Set	910	$85.00 – 90.00
8 pc. Patio Plate and Mug Set	913	$275.00 – 285.00
Mixing Bowl or Open Baker, 5"	915	$35.00 – 40.00
Mixing Bowl or Open Baker, 7"	917	$35.00 – 40.00
Mixing Bowl or Open Baker, 9"	919	$35.00 – 40.00
3 pc. Mixing Bowl or Open Baker	920	$65.00 – 70.00
Creamer Jug	921	$45.00 – 50.00
Salad or Spaghetti Bowl	922	$30.00 – 35.00
Wood Spoon or Fork Set	923	$10.00 – 12.00
9 pc. Salad Set	924	$130.00 – 135.00
Handled Batter Bowl	928	$50.00 – 55.00

CORN WARE

The first seven pieces of Corn Ware were designed in 1941, and given by Proctor and Gamble as premiums. The corn was white in color with green leaves. The ware was oven proof, to enable the consumer to bake and serve.

In 1946 the original White Corn Ware design was changed. The new Corn Ware pieces were slightly larger in size, and the color was changed to yellow corn with green leaves. The sugar shaker was dropped, and many new pieces were added, including prepackaged sets. The new dinnerware line was called Corn King. It was the most successful dinnerware line in Shawnee's history.

By 1954 the Corn King volume of sales had dropped off substantially. John Bonistall, president of Shawnee, decided to change the color to lighter yellow corn and darker green leaves and to add new prepackaged sets. Rather than discontinue the line, the name was changed to Corn Queen, and it was put on display in Shawnee's showroom. Once again, the Corn Ware line was a huge success. Corn Queen remained in production until the plant closed in 1961.

The history of the Corn Ware doesn't end there. After Shawnee was closed, a company by the name of Terrace Ceramics purchased some of the corn line molds. The Terrace corn is slightly smaller, the color was changed to a brown and beige glaze, called Maizeware, and a yellow and green glaze, very different from the Shawnee yellow and green. The Shawnee name was removed from the bottoms of the pieces and replaced with Terrace Ceramics. However, we do occasionally find a piece of Terrace corn ware with the Shawnee name still on it.

Because we were able to provide the Corn King and Corn Queen literature with all the Corn Ware items pictured, we did not include additional photographs of those lines.

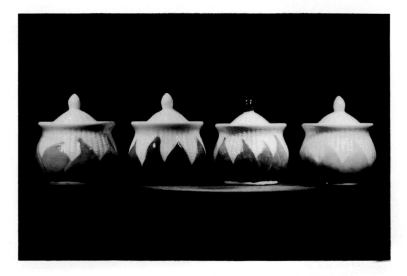

King, Queen, White, Terrace
Note the color differences and the slight size variation.

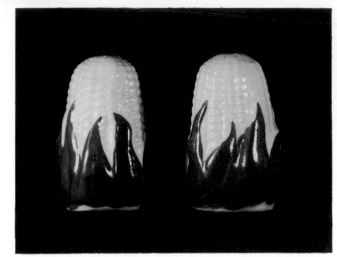

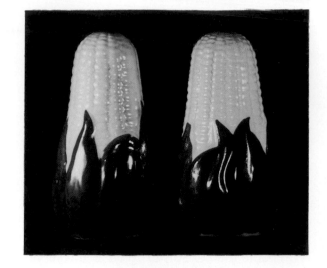

3¹/₄" Salt and Pepper
$25.00 – 30.00

5¹/₄" Salt and Pepper
$30.00 – 35.00

Utility Jar/Sugar Bowl
Marked: USA
$35.00 – 40.00

Sugar Shaker
Marked: USA
$55.00 – 60.00

12 oz. Creamer
Marked: USA
$25.00 – 30.00

40 oz. Jug
Marked: USA
$60.00 – 65.00

30 oz. Tea Pot
Marked: USA
$75.00 – 85.00

Corn King:

5¼" Salt and Pepper		$35.00 – 40.00	10 oz. Tea Pot	Shawnee 65	$165.00 – 175.00
3¼" Salt and Pepper		$26.00 – 28.00	Soup/Cereal Bowl	Shawnee 94	$45.00 – 50.00
Relish Tray	Shawnee 79	$35.00 – 40.00	6" Fruit Dish	Shawnee 92	$40.00 – 45.00
Individual Casserole	Shawnee 73	$125.00 – 150.00	8" Salad Plate	Shawnee 93	$35.00 – 40.00
Covered Butter Dish	Shawnee 72	$50.00 – 55.00	Cup	90	$30.00 – 32.00
Utility Jar or			Saucer	91	$15.00 – 18.00
Sugar Bowl	Shawnee 78	$30.00 – 35.00	10" Plate	Shawnee 68	$35.00 40.00
Creamer	Shawnee 70	$26.00 – 28.00	Three Piece Range Set		$70.00 – 75.00
5" Mixing Bowl	Shawnee 5	$22.00 – 25.00	Cookie Jar	Shawnee 66	$300.00 – 350.00
6½" Mixing bowl	Shawnee 6	$30.00 – 35.00	40 oz. Jug	Shawnee 71	$65.00 – 70.00
8" Mixing Bowl	Shawnee 8	$40.00 – 45.00	Large Casserole	Shawnee 74	$35.00 – 40.00
12" Platter	Shawnee 96	$50.00 – 55.00	8 oz. Mug	Shawnee 69	$45.00 – 50.00
9" Vegetable Dish	Shawnee 95	$50.00 – 55.00	30 oz. Tea Pot	Shawnee 75	$75.00 – 85.00

Corn King Sets:
Polly Ann's Pop Corn $190.00 – 200.00   Town and Country Snack Set $200.00 – 225.00

Corn Queen:
5¼" Salt and Pepper No Mark $35.00 – 40.00
3¼" Salt and Pepper No Mark $26.00 – 28.00

Relish Tray   Shawnee 79 $25.00 – 30.00
Individual Casserole   Shawnee 73 $125.00 – 150.00
Covered Butter Dish   Shawnee 72 $50.00 – 55.00

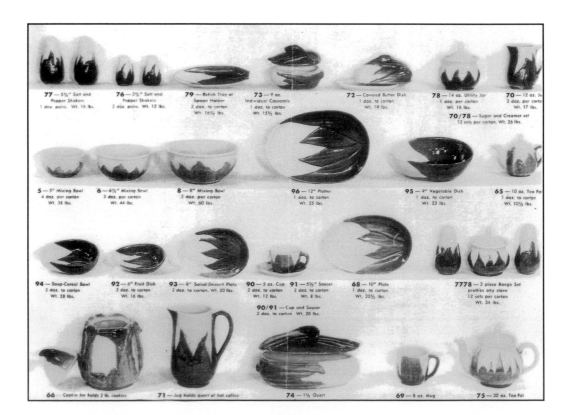

Utility Jar or Sugar Bowl	Shawnee 78	$30.00 – 35.00		10" Plate	Shawnee 68	$35.00 – 40.00
Creamer	Shawnee 70	$24.00 – 26.00		Three Piece Range Set		$110.00 – 115.00
5" Mixing Bowl	Shawnee 5	$20.00 – 22.00		Cookie Jar	Shawnee 66	$300.00 – 350.00
6½" Mixing Bowl	Shawnee 6	$22.00 – 24.00		40 oz. Jug	Shawnee 71	$60.00 – 65.00
8" Mixing Bowl	Shawnee 8	$30.00 – 35.00		Large Casserole	Shawnee 74	$45.00 – 50.00
12" Platter	Shawnee 96	$50.00 – 55.00		8 oz. Mug	Shawnee 69	$45.00 – 50.00
9" Vegetable Dish	Shawnee 95	$50.00 – 55.00		30 oz. Tea Pot	Shawnee 75	$75.00 – 85.00
10 oz. Tea Pot	Shawnee 65	$165.00 – 175.00		Mixing Bowl Set		$100.00 – 110.00
Soup/Cereal Bowl	Shawnee 94	$45.00 – 50.00		Table Set		$100.00 – 110.00
6" Fruit Bowl	Shawnee 92	$40.00 – 45.00		Snack Set		$350.00 – 365.00
8" Salad Plate	Shawnee 93	$30.00 – 35.00		Place Setting		$220.00 – 225.00
Cup	90	$28.00 – 30.00		Pop Corn Set		$190.00 – 200.00
Saucer	91	$15.00 – 18.00		Corn Roast Set		$165.00 – 175.00

MISCELLANEOUS
KITCHENWARE

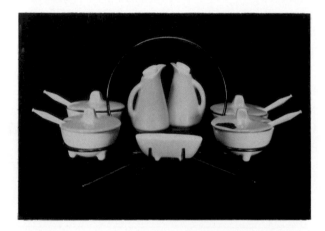

Saucy Susan
$75.00 – 80.00

Top of Saucy Susan Box
$100.00 – 125.00 in original box

Side of Saucy Susan Box

The Saucy Susan consists of a salt and peper, stoppered oil and vinegar cruets, and four individual sauce or preserve cups with covers and servers. It is available in Pink and White, Turquoise and White, and Black and White with copper or brass frames. All of the pieces except the salt and pepper are marked with a USA. They also originally had a Kenwood paper label.

188

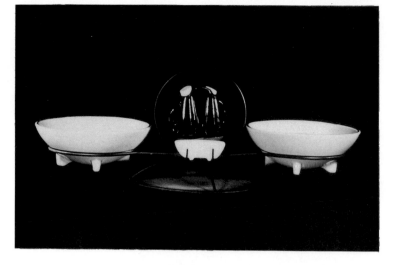

Salad Susan
$90.00 – 100.00

The Salad Susan consists of a salt and pepper, oil and vinegar and two 9" bowls. It comes in Pink or Turquoise accented with Black in a revolving copper frame.

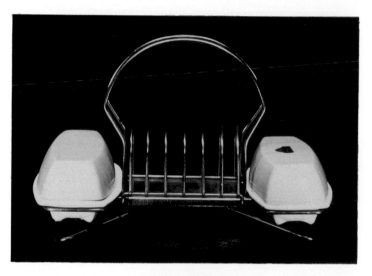

Toastee Susan
$80.00 – 90.00

The Toastee has two covered compartments. One dish is for butter, the other dish has two compartments for preserves. Available in Pink, Turquoise, and Black. The copper or brass rack serves as a napkin holder or toast server.

Supper Susan
$75.00 – 80.00

Supper Susan 18" consists of one-quart chafing dish, small and large serving dishes, and warmer in a triple plated brass frame. Available in decorated Black and White, and decorated Pink and White with Black cover.

Supper Susan 16" consists of the same elements in smaller size. Available in Pink and White and Turquoise and White.

Party Chafing Dish
Marked: Kenwood USA 999
$65.00

Black cover on a vined white casserole and warmer. Stand is triple plated brass.

Patio Carafe
Marked: Kenwood USA 945
$75.00 – 80.00

Carafe, 48 ounce, with white stopper and matching warmer. Stand is triple plated brass.

Sundial Chafing Dish 1 quart
Marked: Kenwood USA 992
$50.00

Sundial Chafing Dish 2 quart
Marked: Kenwood USA 993
$50.00

Brunch Casserole – Chafing Dish
Kenwood USA 940
$55.00 – 65.00

The Sundial casseroles and chafing dishes are available in Pink and Black and Turqouise and Black. Each came with a triple plated brass stand and matching warmer for a candle. Three sizes available: 16 ounce, not shown, marked Kenwood USA 991, a 2 quart and 3 quart.

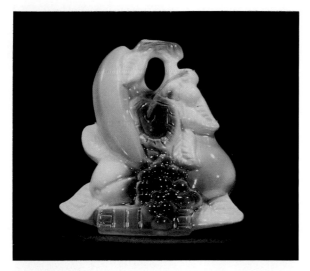

Fruit String Holder
No Mark
$100.00 – 125.00

Ribbed Bowls 5", 6", 7", 8", 9"
Marked: USA
$15.00 – 18.00 each

Brunch Bowls
Marked: Kenwood USA 941 and 942
6", 7", 8" in Yellow, Turquoise, and Pink with Culinary Symbols
$22.00 – 24.00 each

Spoon Rest
Marked: USA
Also available in White
$22.00 – 24.00

The embossed tumblers have been found in Turquoise, Yellow, and Blue. However, more colors may be available. The Stars and Stripes tumbler has been found in Turquoise, Yellow, Old Ivory, Blue, Dark Green, Cobalt Blue, Dark Yellow, and Tangerine.

Fruit Casserole
Marked: Shawnee USA 83
$45.00 – 50.00

Embossed Tumbler 5"
Marked: USA
$6.00 – 8.00

Stars and Stripes Tumbler 3"
Marked: USA
$6.00 – 8.00

Toby Mug
Marked: USA
$25.00 – 30.00

The Pink Elephant has long been collected and displayed as a cookie jar. It is, however, an ice server. It holds two trays of ice cubes and has a plastic seal to hold the cold. It was cold painted with either a White collar or a Black collar. Both the markings of Shawnee 60 and USA Kenwood 60 have been found on it.

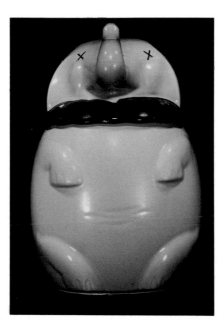

The inside plastic (rubber) seal
Ice Server With Seal
$200.00 – 225.00

Ice Server with White Collar
$200.00 – 250.00

Ice Server with Black Collar
$200.00 – 250.00

Pie Chick
No Mark
$45.00 – 50.00

Pie Chick with Paper Apron
No Mark
$75.00 – 80.00

Over the years, there has been much debate as to whether the Pie Chick is Shawnee or Morton Pottery. We were fortunate enough to find the Pie Chick in a Butler Brothers catalog. It is Shawnee. It could be purchased alone or with an assortment of other Shawnee pieces.

It was also given out by Pillsbury as a premium, accompanied by a cut-out apron with the instructions on how to use it.

The instructions say to cut-out and slip over the Pillsbury Pie Chick's Head.

The apron reads, "Directions for Use: Place Pie-Chick in center of your pie and fit the upper crust snugly around the base above the slots. While the pie is baking, steam will escape thru Pie-Chick, the juices will be kept in and filling will not boil over."

Go-Togethers

The following sets have not been pictured together, but instead the items are shown in their appropriate sections. For easy reference, we have listed the pieces that are available in each set.

Cottage Set
Cookie Jar
Tea Pot
Salt and Pepper
Grease Jar

Cloverbud Set
Smiley Cookie Jar
Winnie Cookie Jar
Tea Pot
Smiley Creamer
Sugar/Grease Jar
Large Smiley and Winnie Salt and Pepper
Small Smiley and Winnie Salt and Pepper
Smiley Pitcher

Fruit Set
Cookie Jar
Ball Jug
Casserole
Sugar/Grease Jar
Large Salt and Pepper, that rest on Sugar
Small Salt and Pepper

Laurel Wreath Pattern Set
5 and 6 Cup Tea Pots
French Drip Coffee Maker
Utility Pitcher
Sugar
Creamer
Grease Jar
Salt and Pepper Shakers

Pennsylvania Dutch Set
Cookie Jar
30, 27, 18, 14, and 10 ounce Tea Pots
Coffee Maker 52 oz.
Coffee Maker – drip style 42 oz.
Ball Jug
Batter Pitcher 34 oz.
Creamer
Sugar
Grease Jar
Salt and Pepper Shakers

Sunflower Set
Ball Jug
Creamer
Sugar
Large and Small Salt and Pepper Shakers
Tea Pot
Coffee Pot

Wave Pattern Set
5 and 6 cup Tea Pots
French Drip Coffee Maker
5½" and 7" Utility Pitchers
Creamer
Sugar
Grease Jar
Salt and Pepper Shakers

Tea Pots

Shawnee began designing and manufacturing tea pots when they opened in 1937 and continued until they closed in 1961. From the late 1930's through the early 1940's, the tea pots had a very simple and utilitarian appearance. In the mid-1940's through 1954, the designs became more figurative and decorative, thus appealing to individuals that would purchase them to decorate with, not necessarily to use. From 1954 through 1961, the only tea pots manufactured were the corn tea pots.

Laurel Wreath 5 Cup
Marked: USA; Blue, Yellow, Green
$45.00 – 50.00

Laurel Wreath 6 Cup
Marked: USA; Blue, Yellow, Green
$45.00 – 50.00

Wave Pattern 5 Cup
Marked: USA; Blue, Yellow, Green
$45.00 – 50.00

Rosette 5 Cup
Marked: USA
$30.00 – 35.00

Rosette 5 Cup
Marked: USA
$30.00 – 35.00

Rosette 5 Cup
Marked: USA
$30.00 – 35.00

The Rosette tea pots date back to 1941. Notice the different finials. They have been found in Dark Green, Cobalt Blue, Peach, Burgundy, Yellow, and Ivory.

Horseshoe Design 8 Cup
Marked: USA; Yellow, Flax Blue, Turquoise
$40.00 – 45.00

Horseshoe Design 7 Cup
Marked: USA, French Drip Type, Yellow, Flax Blue, Turquoise
$60.00 – 65.00

Round Embossed with Horizontal Rings
Marked: USA; Dark Green, Dark Blue, Yellow, Burgundy, White,
$30.00 – 35.00

Drape 4 Cup
Marked USA; Dark Green, Dark Blue, Yellow, Burgundy, White
$30.00 – 35.00

Criss Cross 5 Cup "1942"
Marked: USA; Burgundy, Turquoise, Flax Blue, Dusty Rose
$30.00 – 35.00

Horizontal Ringed 5 Cup
Marked: USA; Dark Green, Cobalt Blue, Yellow, Burgundy
$30.00 – 35.00

Half Criss Cross 5 Cup "1943"
Marked: USA; Yellow, Flax Blue, Turquoise
$30.00 – 35.00

Fern Embossed 8 Cup
Marked: USA; Peach, Yellow, Blue, Green
$50.00 – 60.00

197

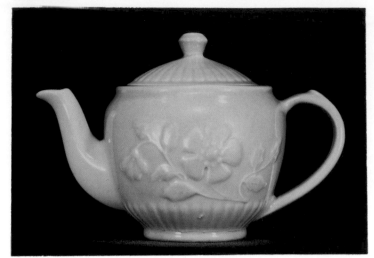

Embossed Flower 8 Cup
Marked: USA; Blue, Yellow, Green, Ribbed Bottom
$30.00 – 35.00

Swirl 6 Cup
Marked: USA; Blue, Green, Yellow
$30.00 – 35.00

Elite – Gold and Decals 4 Cup
Marked: USA
$65.00 – 70.00

Embossed Rose/Gold 6 Cup
USA
$60.00 – 65.00

Embossed Rose – Gold Gilded
Marked: USA
$125.00 – 150.00

Chanticleer – Gold Gilded
Marked: Patented Chanticleer
Rare

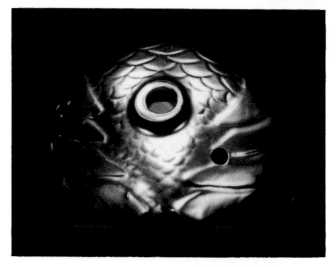

Lid to Chanticleer Tea Pot

Paneled – Gold and Decals 4 Cup
Marked: USA
$55.00 – 60.00

Sunflower – Gold 7 Cup
Marked: USA
$75.00 – 85.00

Clover Bud 7 Cup
Marked: USA
$65.00 – 75.00

Granny Ann – Gold 7 Cup Marked: Patented Granny Ann USA
$200.00+; Green & Lavender Apron Gold & Decals $200.00+;
Plain $150.00 – 175.00

Granny Ann – Gold 7 Cup
Marked: Patented Granny Ann USA
$200.00+

Piper's Son/Gold 5 Cup
Marked: Patented Tom The Pipers Son USA
$150.00 – 160.00

Elephant 5 Cup
Marked: USA
$125.00 – 135.00

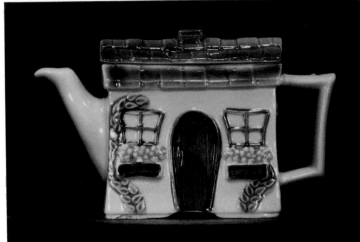

Cottage 5 Cup
Marked: USA 7
$650.00+

Convertional Style #1
Marked: USA; Blue Flower, Blue Bud/Gold
$60.00 – 65.00

Convertional Style #2
Marked: USA; Red Flower/Gold/with Pinky Rest
$60.00 – 65.00

Vertical Ribbed Base
Marked: USA; Red Flower, Red & Blue Bud/Gold
$60.00 – 65.00

Vertical Ribbed Base
Marked: USA; Red Flower, Red Bud/Gold
$60.00 – 65.00

Vertical Ribbed Base
Marked: USA; Blue Tulip Like Flower/Gold
$60.00 – 65.00

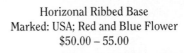

Horizonal Ribbed Base
Marked: USA; Red and Blue Flower
$50.00 – 55.00

Horizonal Ribbed Base
Marked: USA; Red Flower, Blue Bud/Gold
$60.00 – 65.00

Ribbed Collar
Marked: USA; Tulip Flower/Gold
$60.00 – 65.00

Pennsylvania Dutch 30 oz.
Marked: USA
$200.00 – 225.00

Pennsylvania Dutch 27oz.
Marked: USA 27
$75.00 – 80.00

Pennsylvania 18 oz.
Marked: USA 18
$70.00 – 75.00

Pennsylvania Dutch 14 oz.
Marked: USA 14
$65.00 – 70.00

Pennsylvania Dutch 10 oz.
Marked: USA 10
$60.00 – 65.00

Dutch Style 27 oz.
Marked: USA 27
$50.00 – 55.00

Dutch Style 18 oz.
Marked: USA 18
$45.00 – 50.00

Dutch Style 14 oz.
Marked: USA 14
$40.00 – 45.00

Dutch Style 10 oz.
Marked: USA 10
$35.00 – 40.00

The Dutch Style tea pots are available in Blue, Green, and Yellow, plain and with gold trim.

Corn King 30 oz.
Marked: Shawnee 75
$75.00 – 85.00

Corn King 10 oz.
Marked: Shawnee 65
$165.00 – 175.00

Corn Queen & White Corn tea pots are listed in the Cornware Section.

COFFEE MAKERS

Sunflower
Marked: USA
$145.00 – 150.00

Pennsylvania Dutch Style
Marked: USA
$185.00 – 190.00

Dutch Style
Marked: USA
$85.00 – 95.00

Embossed Flower
Marked: USA
$145.00 – 155.00

Not Shown:

Pennsylvania Dutch with Aluminum Coffee Basket	42 oz.	$150.00 – 175.00
Pennsylvania Dutch without Coffee Basket	52 oz.	$145.00 – 150.00

AFTER DINNER (A.D.) COFFEE POTS

Ribbed
Marked: USA
$35.00 – 45.00

Ribbed with Rosette Lid
Marked: USA
$30.00 – 35.00

We believe this to be the wrong lid; however, it fits and
was purchased this way.

The A.D. Coffee Pots come in Dark Green, Cobalt Blue, Yellow, and Burgundy.

CREAMERS

Wave Pattern
Marked: USA; Yellow, Blue, Green
$20.00 – 22.00

Laurel Wreath
Marked: USA; Yellow, Blue, Green
$20.00 – 22.00

Sunflower
Marked: USA; Embossed Sunflower
$50.00 – 55.00

Pennsylvania Dutch
Marked: USA 12; Decorated with Heart and Flowers
$55.00 – 60.00

Pennsylvania Dutch
Marked: USA 10; Decorated with Heart and Flowers
$55.00 – 60.00

Dutch Style/Gold & Decals
Marked: USA 10; Yellow, Blue, Green
$55.00 – 60.00

Dutch Style
Marked: USA 12; Decorated with Red Feather
$35.00 – 40.00

Dutch Style
Marked: USA 12; Yellow, Blue, Green
$25.00 – 30.00

Tulip
Marked: USA
$75.00 – 80.00

Lobster
Marked: USA 909
$75.00 – 80.00

Smiley/Gold
Marked: Patented Smiley USA; Embossed Cloverbud
$150.00 – 165.00

Smiley/Gold Gilded
Marked: Patented Smiley USA
$375.00 – 400.00

Puss'n Boots/Gold
Marked: Shawnee USA 85
$100.00 – 125.00

Puss'n Boots/Gold
Marked: Pat. Puss'n Boots USA
$100.00 – 125.00

Puss'n Boots
Marked: USA 85
$100.00 – 125.00

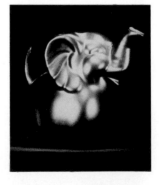

Elephant/Gold and Decals
Marked: Pat. USA
$325.00 – 350.00

Elephant/Gold Gilded
Marked: Pat. USA
$375.00 – 400.00

Other pieces available:

Smiley	Embossed Flower	No Gold	$30.00 – 35.00	Gold	$150.00 – 175.00
Puss'n Boots	White with Red Bow	No Gold	$22.00 – 24.00	Gold	$150.00 – 175.00
Puss'n Boots	Yellow	No Gold	$30.00 – 35.00		
Elephant	White with Red Ears	No Gold	$20.00 – 22.00		

SUGARS

Wave Pattern/Open
Marked: USA; Yellow, Blue, Green
$22.00 – 24.00

Laurel Wreath/Open
Marked: USA; Yellow, Blue, Green
$22.00 – 24.00

Sunflower/With Lid
Marked: USA; Embossed Sunflower
$50.00 – 55.00

Pennsylvania Dutch/Open
Marked: USA; Decorated With Heart and Flowers
$50.00 – 55.00

Dutch Style/Open/Gold and Decals
Marked: USA; Yellow, Blue, Green
$55.00 – 60.00

Dutch Style/Open
Marked: USA; Yellow, Blue, Green
$25.00 – 30.00

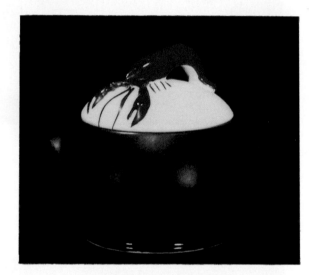

Lobster Sugar/Utility Jar
Marked: Kenwood USA 907
$30.00 – 35.00

Fruit Sugar/Utility Jar
Marked: Shawnee 81
$35.00 – 40.00

Cloverbud Sugar/Utility Jar
Marked: USA
$50.00 – 55.00

UTILITY JARS

Covered Utility Basket, Round
Marked: USA
$50.00 – 55.00

Covered Utility Basket/Gold, Oval
Marked: USA
$100.00 – 110.00

Covered Utility Bucket/Gold, Round
Marked: USA
$80.00 – 85.00

Covered Utility Basket/Gold, Oval
Marked: USA
$110.00 – 120.00

GREASE JARS

The Grease Jars were normally sold in a three piece set, which included a salt and pepper shaker. These sets were called range sets.

Wave Pattern With Lid
Marked: USA; Yellow, Blue, Green
$28.00 – 30.00

Laurel Wreath With Lid
Marked: USA; Yellow, Blue, Green
$28.00 – 30.00

Decorator With Lid
Marked: USA
$50.00 – 55.00

Pennsylvania Dutch With Lid
Marked: USA; Decorated with Heart and Flowers
$65.00 – 75.00

Dutch Style With Lid
Marked: USA; Yellow, Blue, Green
$30.00 – 35.00

Cottage
Marked: USA 8
$350.00 – 375.00

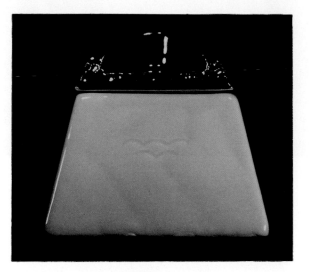

Sahara
Marked: Kenwood USA 977
$50.00 – 55.00

Sahara Range Set in Box
$125.00 – 130.00

213

PITCHERS

Wave Pattern 5½"
Marked: USA; Yellow, Blue, Green
$22.00 – 24.00

Wave Pattern 7"
Marked: USA; Yellow, Blue, Green
$24.00 – 26.00

Laurel Wreath
Marked: USA; Yellow, Blue, Green
$22.00 – 24.00

Ribbed Utility
Marked: USA; Blue, Turquoise, Antique White, Yellow
$16.00 – 18.00

Stars and Stripes
Marked: USA; Yellow, Old Ivory, Blue, Dark Green, Cobalt Blue, Tangerine
$16.00 – 18.00

Space Saver Jug 20 oz.
Marked: USA 40; Embossed Flower
$24.00 – 26.00

Space Saver Jug 20 oz.
Marked: USA 35; Flower Decorated
$22.00 – 24.00

Bo Peep Jug/Gold 30 oz.
Marked: Shawnee USA 47
$150.00 – 175.00

Boy Blue Jug/Gold 20 oz.
Marked: Shawnee 46
$175.00 – 200.00

Bo Peep Jug 40 oz.
Marked: USA Pat. Bo Peep
$85.00 – 90.00

Chanticleer
Marked: Patented Chanticleer USA
$55.00 – 60.00

Chanticleer Gold and Decal
Marked: Patented Chanticleer USA
$350.00 – 400.00

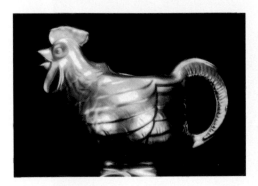

Chanticleer Gold Gilded
Marked: Patented Chanticleer USA
$400.00 – 450.00

Smiley/Gold
Marked: Pat. Smiley USA;
Embossed Flowers
$175.00 – 200.00

Smiley
Marked: Pat. Smiley USA;
Embossed Cloverbud
$175.00 – 200.00

Fruit Ball Jug 48 oz.
Shawnee 80
$75.00 – 80.00
Pennsylvania Ball Jug
$85.00 – 90.00

Sunflower Ball Jug 48 oz.
Marked: USA
$75.00 – 80.00

Tulip Ball Jug 48 oz.
Marked: USA
$100.00 – 105.00

SALT AND PEPPERS

The salt and pepper shakers have become very popular among collectors. Although many of the shakers were poured from identical molds, the avid collectors are always searching for a different color or decal variation.

We have been asked many times how the Shawnee shakers were originally paired. The salt shaker will have bigger or more holes, due to the coarse texture of the salt. Pepper is usually finely ground, so the pepper shaker will have fewer or smaller holes. It is fairly safe to say that if you have a set of shakers with the same number of holes, or the same size, that you have two salts or two peppers. Shawnee shakers range from 3¼" to 5½" (which are often referred to as range size). The larger ones have four and five holes, and the smaller ones have three and four holes. However, as with most Shawnee Pottery, there are a few exceptions to the rules, which we have noted.

There has always been some question as to how the Smiley and Winnie shakers were paired. Smileys were produced first, and paired according to the number of holes. Later, Winnie was introduced and was paired with a Smiley. To know which Winnie and Smiley go together, match Winnie's top coat button to Smiley's neckerchief, and if the holes are as stated above, you have a pair!

Shawnee offered their retailers an assortment pack, containing various pieces of pottery, which included the small Boy Blue and Bo Peep shakers. In this pack, the pottery was arranged in bins, and the customers would pair the Boy Blue and Bo Peep shakers the way they wanted. However, the proper way to pair these shakers is with a three and four hole, because that is how they were originally designed to be paired.

Large Salt and Peppers:

Smileys
Green Neckerchief
$125.00 – 135.00

Smileys
Red Neckerchief
$125.00 – 135.00

Smileys
Peach Neckerchief
$125.00 – 135.00

Smileys
Green Neckerchief - Gold & Decals
$175.00 – 180.00

Smileys
Blue Neckerchief
$125.00 – 135.00

Smileys
Blue Neckerchief - Gold & Decals
$175.00 – 180.00

Smiley and Winnie/Heart Set
$165.00 – 175.00

Smiley and Winnie/Clover Bud Set
$200.00 – 235.00

Dutch Kids
Blue
$25.00 – 30.00

Dutch Kids
Blue, Gold
$65.00 – 75.00

Dutch Kids
Brown
$30.00 – 35.00

Dutch Kids
Brown/Gold
$65.00 – 75.00

Jack and Jill
$45.00 – 55.00

Jack and Jill
Gold & Decals
$200.00 – 225.00

Jill: Decorated like Great Northern Jar
Jack: Not Shown; decorated the same
$350.00 – 375.00 for pair

Swiss Kids
$40.00 – 45.00

Swiss Kids/Gold
$60.00 – 65.00

Chanticleers
$45.00 – 50.00

Chanticleers
Gold and Decorated
$170.00 – 180.00

Fruit
Made to sit along Fruit Sugar Bowl
$35.00 – 40.00

Muggsy
$175.00+

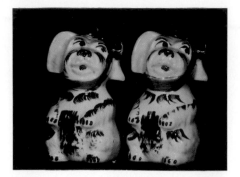

Muggsy
Gold and Decals
$400.00+

Pennsylvania Dutch
$90.00 – 100.00
Not Shown: Dutch Style, Yellow,
Blue, and Green $45.00 – 50.00

Sunflower
$40.00 – 45.00

Decorator Front and Back
$70.00 – 75.00

Decorator Front and Back
$70.00 – 75.00

Wave Pattern
Yellow, Blue, Green
$40.00 – 45.00

Laurel Wreath
Yellow, Blue, Green
$25.00 – 30.00

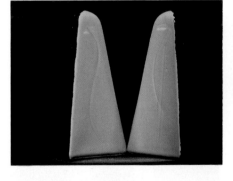

Sahara
Pink, Turquoise
$25.00 – 30.00

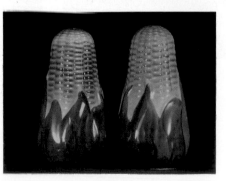

White Corn
Gold
$200.00 – 225.00

Small Salt and Peppers:

Farmer Pigs
$75.00 – 80.00

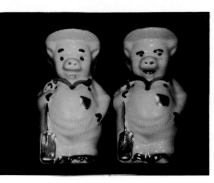

Farmer Pigs/Gold
$100.00 – 110.00

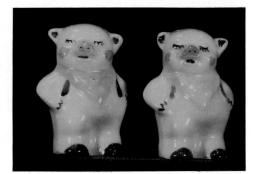

Smileys
Pointed Neckerchief
$65.00 – 75.00

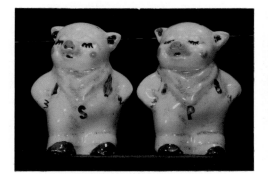

Smileys
Gold Pointed Neckerchief
$90.00 – 100.00

Smileys
Peach Neckerchief
$45.00 – 50.00

Smileys/Gold
Peach Neckerchief
$55.00 – 65.00

Winnie and Smiley/Clover Bud
$75.00 – 85.00

Winnie and Smiley/Heart Set
$55.00 – 60.00

Smiley and Winnie/Gold
$70.00 – 80.00

Smileys
Blue Neckerchief
$30.00 – 35.00

Watering Cans
$24.00 – 26.00

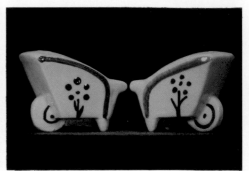

Wheelbarrows
$24.00 – 26.00

Wheelbarrows/Gold
$100.00 – 110.00

Flower Pots
$24.00 – 26.00

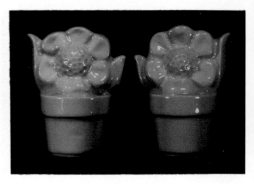

Flower Pots
All White
$50.00 – 55.00

Flower Pots
All Gold Center
$55.00 – 60.00

Flower Pots
Gold Pot & Flower
$50.00 – 55.00

Flower Pots
Gold Trim Flower
$50.00 – 55.00

Fruit
$25.00 – 30.00

Puss'n Boots
$30.00 – 35.00

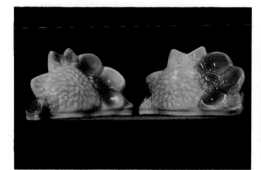

Flower Cluster
$20.00 – 25.00

Flower Cluster
Gold
$55.00 – 60.00

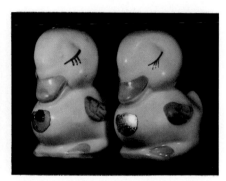

Ducks
$25.00 – 30.00

Sunflower
$30.00 – 35.00

Muggsy
$55.00 – 60.00

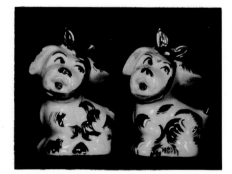

Muggsy/Gold
$175.00 – 200.00

Puss'n Boots
Gold
$125.00 – 150.00

Chanticleers
$30.00 – 35.00

Chanticleers
Gold
$125.00 – 165.00

Owls, Green eyes; $30.00 – 35.00
Owls, Blue eyes; $25.00 – 30.00

Owls
Gold
$70.00 – 80.00

Milk Cans
$30.00 – 35.00

Milk Cans
Gold
$100.00 – 125.00

Jumbo
$95.00 – 100.00

Jumbo – Back

Boy Blue and Bo Peep
$25.00 – 30.00

Boy Blue and Bo Peep
Gold
$50.00 – 55.00

Cottage
$350.00 – 375.00

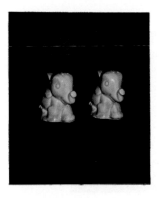

Elephants
White, Turquoise, Flax Blue
$20.00 – 25.00

S & P
$20.00 – 25.00

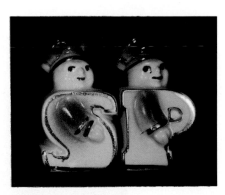

S & P Gold
$40.00 – 45.00

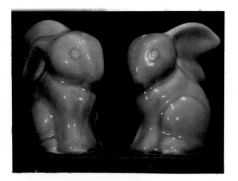

Rabbits – 2 & 3 Holes
White, Turquoise, Dusty Rose, Flax Blue
$20.00 – 25.00

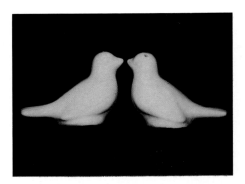

Birds Heads Up – 1 & 2 Holes
White, Turquoise, Dusty Rose
$20.00 – 25.00

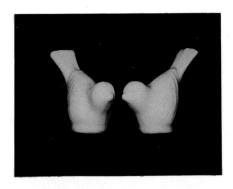

Birds Heads Down – 1 & 2 Holes
White, Turquoise, Dusty Rose
$20.00 – 25.00

Jugs – 2 & 3 Holes
White, Ivory, Rose
$20.00 – 25.00

Ewers – 2 & 3 Holes
White, Ivory, Rose
$20.00 – 25.00

Embossed Jugs – 2 & 3 Holes
White, Ivory, Rose
$20.00 – 25.00

Conventional Design Blocks
$20.00 – 25.00

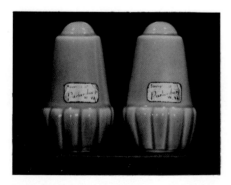

Conventional Design, Ribbed Bottom
$20.00 – 25.00

Conventional Design, Ribbed
$20.00 – 25.00

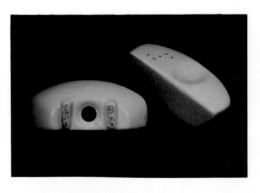

Saucy Shakers
$20.00 – 25.00

CANISTERS

The canisters were first introduced in the late 1930's and were discontinued in October 1942. Their retail price was $11.20 per dozen! They have a plain design and were originally produced with a decal decoration on one side; however, many have turned up with hand painted designs, also. They have a two quart capacity and are available in Turquoise, Flax Blue, and Yellow.

Hand Painted/Gold, 2 qt.
Marked: USA
$75.00 – 100.00

No Decoration, 2 qt.
Marked: USA
$45.00 – 50.00

Hand Painted/Gold, 2 qt.
Marked: USA
$55.00 – 60.00

Dutch Decal, 2 qt.
Marked: USA
$45.00 – 50.00

Dutch Decal, 2 qt.
Marked: USA
$45.00 – 50.00

Fruit Decal, 2 qt.
Marked: USA
$50.00 – 55.00

Fruit Decal, 2 qt.
Marked: USA
$50.00 – 55.00

Canister 1 qt.
Marked: USA; White, Turquoise,
Flax Blue, Yellow
$55.00 – 60.00

COOKIE JARS

Shawnee's first cookie jar was designed in 1937 for the Valencia dinnerware line. From that time until the early 1940's several jars were produced, but they were not the figural type of jars for which Shawnee is so well known. They were very plain, designed to serve as canisters as well as cookie jars. There were also canisters produced and sold as such. Many collectors refer to the canisters as cookie jars. In this section we have differentiated between the two. Where information was available, we also identified and labeled the jars with their proper names.

In 1942 Rudy Ganz, chief designer at Shawnee, was looking through a child's picture book. He came across a pig in overalls with his head cocked and a mischievous half smile. It struck the designer as funny. With the help of Ed Hazel, a member of Ganz's design staff, they made a sculpture. Their first thought was salt and pepper shakers, but they decided a cookie jar would make the best use of the design. They called the cookie jar the "Smiling Pig." It was an immediate success. Many molds were made and thousands upon thousands of the "Smiling Pig" jars were made. It could be purchased with a red or blue neckerchief. The entire output was contracted by Butler Brothers and featured in color on the back of their catalog, along with Smiley's companion pieces, the salt and pepper shakers.

Although the Smiling Pig (Smiley) was the most popular, there were four other cookie jar designs being produced at the same time: Jumbo, which we know as Lucky Elephant, Jack Tar (Sailor boy), and Jack and Jill (Dutch boy and girl). These jars were all hand decorated with cold paint (which is paint applied over the glaze) and could be purchased from $17.00 – $22.00 per dozen. Those certainly were the good 'ole days!

Shawnee jars are not only desired by Shawnee collectors but by cookie jar collectors as well. Because of the demand for these jars, prices have soared over the last couple of years. As with most jars, the gold trimmed are most in demand. However, the gold trim and/or decals were not done at the Shawnee factory. Oddly enough, the most highly sought Shawnee jars today were actually seconds at the time of production. They were jars that did not pass inspection. They may have had glaze misses, chips, dents, or any other kind of imperfection. These rejected jars were sold to decorators. They, in turn, would fire on gold trim, decals, painted patches, flowers, bugs, or hair to camouflage the imperfection. The jars were then sold to speciality stores at higher prices, because now they were hand decorated and gold trimmed.

The rest is history. Shawnee produced many cookie jars after Smiley's debut, each one with a personality all its own.

Cookie Jar facts:

Jack (Dutch Boy)	Patent applied for 1942
Jill (Dutch Girl)	Patent applied for 1942
Smiley	Patent applied for 1942
Jumbo	Patent applied for 1942
Jack Tar (Sailor)	Patent applied for 1942
Muggsy	Patent applied for 1944
Owl	Patent applied for 1944
Puss'n Boots	Patent applied for 1945
Winnie	Patent applied for 1945
Chef	Patent applied for 1948
Drummer	Patent applied for 1948

The proper name for the Sailor Cookie Jar is Jack Tar.
The proper name for the Clown Cookie Jar is Jo Jo.
The proper name for the Dutch Girl Cookie Jar is Jill.
The proper name for the Dutch Boy Cookie Jar is Jack.
The proper name for the Sitting Elephant Cookie Jar is Jumbo.
The proper name for the Drummer Boy Cookie Jar is Drum Major.

The word *gob* on the Jack Tar Cookie Jar has a complicated derivation. According to an article from the Naval Institute Press, the word *gob* is probably an abbreviation for the Spanish word *Captain*, pronounced "Gob-bid-dan" by people in Canton and Hong Kong. This is how they referred to captains of foreign ships, and loosely, to all foreign sailors on their ships or ashore, in the ports of South China. The longer word was then shortened to the first syllable, "gob."

The Smiley Cookie Jars average 11¼" tall.

Chrysanthemum Smiley
Marked: USA
$400.00 – 450.00

Chrysanthemum Smiley/Gold
Marked: USA
$700.00 – 800.00

Tulip Smiley
Marked: USA
$525.00 – 600.00

Clover Bud Smiley
Marked: Pat. Smiley USA
$600.00 – 650.00

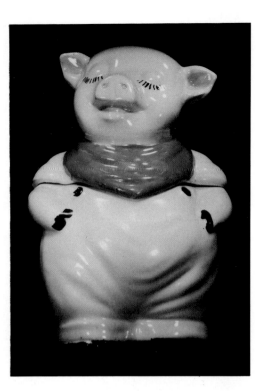

Smiley, Blue Neckerchief
Marked: USA
$150.00 – 175.00

Smiley, Blue Neckerchief, Black Feet
Marked: USA
$180.00 – 200.00

Smiley, Blue Neckerchief, Gold and Decals
Marked: USA
$650.00 – 700.00

Smiley, Blue Neckerchief, Gold and Decals
Marked: USA
650.00 – 700.00

Smiley, Green Neckerchief
Marked: USA
$180.00 – 200.00

Shamrock Smiley
Marked: USA
$400.00 – 450.00

Shamrock Smiley, Gold and Decals
Marked: USA
$600.00 – 650.00

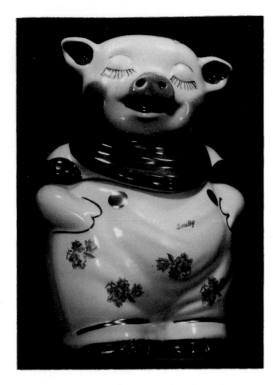

Smiley with Roses, Gold and Decals
Marked: USA
$650.00 – 700.00

Smiley with Roses, Gold and Decals
Marked: USA
$650.00 – 700.00

Smiley, Red Neckerchief, Gold and Decals
Marked: USA
$625.00 – 650.00

Smiley, Yellow Neckerchief, Gold and Decals
Marked: USA
$500.00 – 525.00

Smiley, Yellow Neckerchief
Marked: USA
$150.00 – 175.00

Shamrock Smiley with Butterfly/Gold
Marked: USA
$1,300.00 – 1,325.00

Smiley Head with Butterfly

Smiley with Hair Gold & Decals
Marked: USA
$1,200.00 – 1,225.00

Smiley Head with Hair

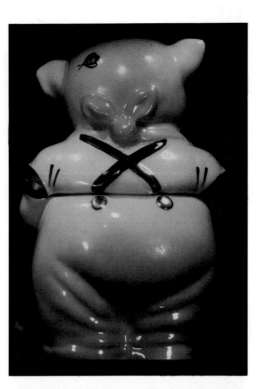

Smiley with Fly, Gold and Decals
Marked: USA
$750.00 – 800.00

Other pieces available:
Smiley with Strawberries $500.00 – 550.00

Smiley with Apples$1,000.00 – 1,100.00
Smiley with Plums$1,000.00 – 1,100.00

Smiley with Fly, Gold and Decals
Marked: USA
$750.00 – 800.00

Smiley with Bee, Gold and Decals
Marked: USA
$750.00 – 800.00

Winnie Cookie Jars average 11½" tall.

Winnie with Blue Collar
Marked: USA
$375.00 – 425.00

Clover Bud Winnie
Marked: Pat Winnie USA
$700.00 – 800.00

Shamrock Winnie
Marked: USA
$375.00 – 425.00

Shamrock Winnie, Red Collar, Gold
Marked: USA
$1,100.00 – 1,200.00

Winnie with Peach Collar
Marked: USA
$375.00 – 425.00

Winnie with Peach Collar, Gold
Marked: USA
$900.00 – 1,100.00

Not shown: Winnie with Apples $525.00 – 550.00

What most collectors know as the "Dutch Boy," was actually named Jack by Shawnee. Jack is 12" tall.

Jack with Striped Pants
Marked: USA
$190.00 – 200.00

Jack with Double Striped Pants
Marked: USA
$550.00 – 600.00

Jack with Striped Pants, Gold and Decals
Marked: USA
$400.00 – 450.00

Jack with Gold and Decals
Marked: USA
$450.00 – 475.00

Jack with Gold and Decals
Marked: USA
$450.00 – 475.00

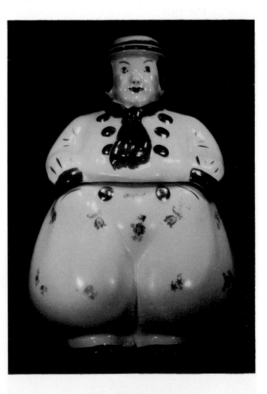

Jack with Gold and Decals
Marked: USA
$450.00 – 475.00

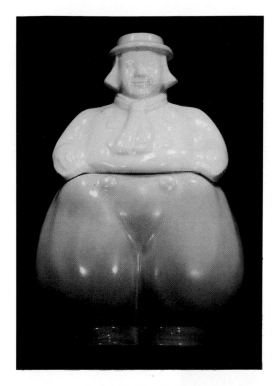

Jack with Blue Pants
Marked: USA
$100.00 – 125.00

Jack with Blue Pants and Patches and Gold
Marked: USA
$500.00 – 525.00

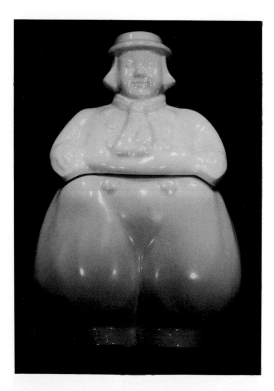

Jack with Yellow Pants
Marked: USA
$100.00 – 125.00

Jack with Yellow Pants and Patches and Gold
Marked: USA
$525.00 – 550.00

What collectors know as the "The Dutch Girl" was named Jill at Shawnee. Jill is 12" tall.

Jill with Tulip
Marked: USA
$250.00 – 275.00

Jill with Tulip, Gold and Decals
Marked: USA
$350.00 – 375.00

Jill with Tulip, Gold and Decals
Marked: USA
$375.00 – 400.00

Jill with Blue Skirt
Marked: USA
$100.00 – 125.00

Jill with Gold and Decals
Marked: USA
$350.00 – 375.00

Jill with Yellow Skirt, Gold and Decals
Marked: USA
$350.00 – 400.00

Jill with Yellow Skirt, Gold and Decals
Marked: USA
$350.00 – 400.00

Jill with Blue Skirt, Gold and Decals
Marked: USA
$350.00 – 375.00

Jill with Blue Skirt, Gold and Decals
Marked: USA
$375.00 – 400.00

Jill with Yellow Skirt
Marked: USA
$100.00 – 125.00

The Great Northern Jars ar 10¾" tall. They were made and given as premiums.

Great Northern Girl, In White
Marked: Great Northern USA 1026
$400.00 – 475.00

Great Northern Girl, Dark Green
Marked: Great Northern USA 1026
$475.00 – 500.00

Great Northern Boy
Marked: Great Northern USA 1025
$475.00 – 500.00

Smiley Cookie Jar Bank
Chocolate Brown Bottom 11¼", Gold
Marked: Patented Smiley Shawnee USA 60
$850.00 – 875.00

Smiley Cookie Jar Bank
Chocolate Brown Bottom 11¼"
Marked: Patented Smiley Shawnee USA 60
$550.00 – 575.00

Smiley Cookie Jar Bank,
Butterscotch Brown Bottom 11¼"
Marked: Patented Smiley Shawnee USA 60
$550.00 – 575.00

Winnie Cookie Jar Bank
Butterscotch Bottom 11½"
Marked: Patented Winnie Shawnee USA 61
$550.00 – 575.00

Winnie Cookie Jar Bank, Gold
Butterscotch Bottom 11½"
Marked: Patented Winnie Shawnee USA 61
$900.00 – 1,000.00

Winnie Cookie Jar Bank, Gold
Chocolate Brown Bottom 11½"
Marked: Patented Winnie Shawnee USA 61
$900.00 – 1,000.00

Winnie Cookie Jar Bank
No Money Slot in Head
$600.00 – 625.00

Bottom of Green Winnie

Winnie Cookie Jar Bank, Green
$1,200.00+
This jar is shown with the wrong head

Muggsy, 11¾"
Marked: Patented Muggsy USA
$550.00 – 600.00

Muggsy, Gold and Decals, 11¾"
Marked: Patented Muggsy USA,
May be found just marked USA
$1,000.00 – 1,100.00

Not shown: Muggsy with Green Bow $1,600.00–1,800.00

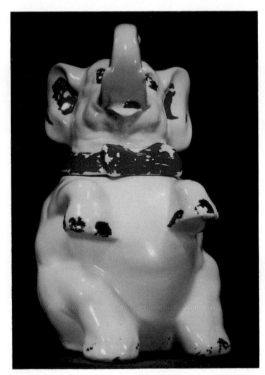

Jumbo, Cold Paint, 12", Red or Blue Bow Tie
Marked: USA
$200.00 – 250.00

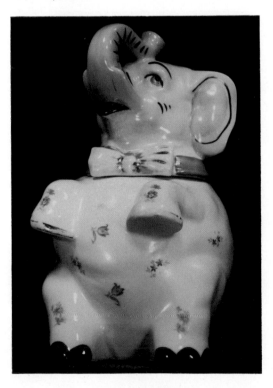

Jumbo, Gold and Decals, 12"
Marked: USA
$950.00 – 1,000.00

Owl 11¹/₂"
Marked: USA
$150.00 – 175.00

Owl, Gold and Decals, 11¹/₂"
Marked: USA
$350.00 – 375.00

Puss'n Boots, Gold and Decals, 10¹/₄", Short Tail
Marked: Patented Puss'n Boots
$700.00 – 800.00

Puss'n Boots, Gold and Decals, 10¹/₄", Short Tail
Marked: Patented Puss'n Boots
$550.00 – 600.00

Puss'n Boots, 10¼", Long Tail
Marked: Patented Puss'n Boots
$200.00 – 225.00

Puss'n Boots, 10¼", Short Tail
Marked: Patented Puss'n Boots
$175.00 – 200.00

Puss'n Boots, Gold and Decals, 10¼", Long Tail
Marked: Patented Puss'n Boots
$625.00 – 650.00

Jack Tar, Cold Paint, 12"
Marked: USA
$150.00 – 200.00

Jack Tar, Gold and Decals, 12", Blond Hair
Marked: USA
$1,200.00 – 1,400.00

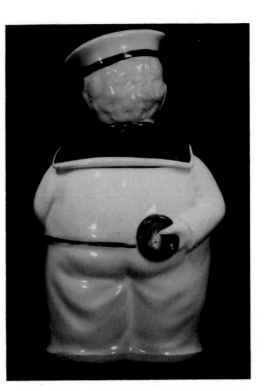

Back of Jack Tar Cookie Jar
Holding a Cookie

Jack Tar, Gold, 12", Black Hair
Marked: USA
$1,100.00 – 1,150.00

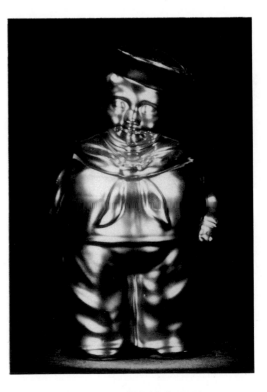

Jack Tar, Gold Gilded, 11¾"
Marked: USA
Rare

Drum Major 10"
Marked: USA 10
$575.00 – 600.00

Jo Jo the Clown 9½"
Marked: Shawnee 12
$475.00 – 500.00

Fruit Basket 8"
Marked: Shawnee 84
$225.00 – 250.00

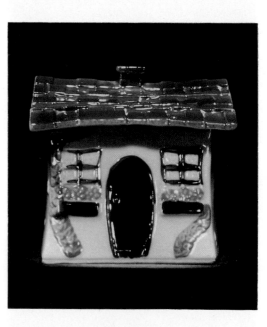

Cottage 6¾"
Marked: USA 6
$1500.00+

Pennsylvania Dutch 8¹/₄"
Marked: USA
$275.00 – 300.00

Dutch Style, Green 8¹/₄"
Marked: USA
$145.00 – 165.00

Dutch Style, Yellow 8¹/₄"
Marked: USA
$145.00 – 165.00

Dutch Style, Blue 8¹/₄", Hand Decorated
Marked: USA
$175.00 – 185.00

Little Chef, 8¹/₂", Multi-color
Marked: USA
$150.00 – 175.00

Little Chef, Gold, 8¹/₂"
Marked: USA
White and Gold
$300.00 – 325.00

Little Chef, Yellow
Marked: USA
$175.00 – 200.00

Little Chef, 8¹/₂", Caramel
Marked: USA
$175.00 – 200.00

Little Chef, Green, 8½"
Marked: USA
$175.00 – 200.00

Basketweave with Decal, 7½"
Marked: USA
$125.00 – 150.00

Basketweave with Decal, 7½"
Marked: USA
$125.00 – 150.00

Basketweave with Decal 7½"
Marked: USA
$125.00 – 150.00

Basketweave, Hand decorated, Gold, 7¹/₂"
Marked: USA
$150.00 – 175.00

Basketweave 7¹/₂"
Marked: USA
$65.00 – 75.00

Corn King 10¹/₂"
Marked: Shawnee #66
$300.00 – 350.00

Corn Queen 10¹/₄"
Marked: Shawnee #66
$300.00 – 350.00

BIBLIOGRAPHY

Vanderbilt, Duane and Janice, *The Collectors Guide to Shawnee Pottery*. Collector Books, Paducah, Kentucky.

Supnick, Mark, *Collecting Shawnee Pottery*. L-W Book Sales, Gas City, Indiana.

Roerig, Fred and Joyce, *The Collectors Encyclopedia of Cookie Jars*. Collector Books, Paducah, Kentucky.

Patent and Trademark Office, patent information

Mangus, Jim and Beverly, private collection of company brochure pages, price guides, company photographs, and articles.

Naval Institute Press, *Naval Ceremonies, Customs and Traditions*, 5th Edition.

Schroeder's
ANTIQUES
Price Guide

. . . is the #1 best-selling antiques & collectibles value guide on the market today, and here's why . . .

Identification & Values Of Over 50,000 Antiques & Collectibles

8½ x 11, 608 Pages, $12.95

• More than 300 advisors, well-known dealers, and top-notch collectors work together with our editors to bring you accurate information regarding pricing and identification.

• More than 45,000 items in almost 500 categories are listed along with hundreds of sharp original photos that illustrate not only the rare and unusual, but the common, popular collectibles as well.

• Each large close-up shot shows important details clearly. Every subject is represented with histories and background information, a feature not found in any of our competitors' publications.

• Our editors keep abreast of newly developing trends, often adding several new categories a year as the need arises.

If it merits the interest of today's collector, you'll find it in *Schroeder's*. And you can feel confident that the information we publish is up to date and accurate. Our advisors thoroughly check each category to spot inconsistencies, listings that may not be entirely reflective of market dealings, and lines too vague to be of merit. Only the best of the lot remains for publication.

Without doubt, you'll find
SCHROEDER'S ANTIQUES PRICE GUIDE
the only one to buy for
reliable information and values.

COLLECTOR BOOKS
A Division of Schroeder Publishing Co., Inc.